Saving For The Future: For Black Women

By Michaela Dosunmu

Disclaimer:

The information contained in this book is for educational and informational purposes only. It is not intended as a substitute for professional advice, whether medical, psychological, financial, or otherwise. The author is not a licensed healthcare or mental health professional. Readers should seek advice from their physician, therapist, or other qualified professionals for any personal concerns related to health, habits, or behavior change.

While the practices and techniques discussed in this book are based on research and the author's experiences, individual results may vary. The recommendations in this book should be considered complementary to conventional medical, psychological, or professional care, and not as a replacement.

The author and publisher disclaim any liability for any direct or indirect consequences arising from the use of the information in this book. It is essential to consult with a qualified professional before implementing any significant lifestyle or behavioral changes, especially if you have a medical condition or specific personal circumstances.

By reading this book, you acknowledge that the information is not intended to diagnose or treat any condition and is provided on an "as-is" basis.

Table Of Contents

Introduction

Taking Control of Your Financial Future

When you think about your financial future, how does it make you feel? Does it seem exciting, daunting, or maybe even out of reach? The truth is, no matter where you're starting from, taking control of your finances is possible—and it begins with one simple, powerful habit: saving.

Saving isn't just about setting money aside; it's about creating opportunities, building stability, and paving the way for the life you want. It's about empowerment, independence, and saying yes to your future.

Why Saving Matters

Saving gives you options. It's what lets you breathe a little easier when life throws you a curveball, like an unexpected medical bill or a car repair. It's the freedom to make choices—not based on fear or scarcity, but on what truly matters to you. Imagine having a financial cushion that allows you to take a career leap, start a business, or give your child the education they deserve. That's the power of saving.

But saving isn't just about the immediate benefits—it's about building a legacy. For Black women, saving has an even deeper significance. It's a step toward breaking cycles of financial struggle and creating generational wealth. It's about ensuring that your family and future generations have opportunities and resources that weren't always available to you. Every dollar saved is a dollar that builds your legacy.

Think about your dreams. What would financial security mean for you? Is it peace of mind? The ability to retire comfortably? The chance to give back to your community? No matter the dream, saving is the bridge that connects today's effort to tomorrow's possibilities.

Challenges Black Women Face in Building Wealth

Let's talk about the barriers. You've probably felt the weight of systemic inequalities, whether it's wage gaps, limited access to resources, or the pressure to prioritize everyone else's needs over your own. As a Black woman, the journey to financial stability can feel unfairly steep, with fewer opportunities and more responsibilities.

On average, Black women earn less than their counterparts, making it harder to save, invest, and build wealth. Add to that the cost of student loans, childcare, or supporting extended family, and the path forward can seem overwhelming. These challenges are real—but they are not insurmountable.

Your resilience is your strength. Despite these obstacles, Black women have always found ways to thrive, innovate, and support one another. This book is here to help you turn that resilience into financial empowerment. It's not about ignoring the challenges but about equipping yourself with the tools to overcome them.

Another common challenge is the emotional and cultural weight of money. You might feel guilty about prioritizing your financial goals when family or community needs arise. But remember this: taking care of your finances is not selfish. In fact, it's one of the most selfless things you can do. By creating a strong financial foundation, you position yourself to help others without sacrificing your own stability.

Empowerment Through Financial Planning

Imagine knowing exactly where your money is going each month. Picture the confidence of watching your savings grow steadily, even if it's just a little at a time. Financial planning is about more than crunching numbers—it's about taking control. It's about telling your money where to go instead of wondering where it went.

What does financial empowerment look like to you? Is it an emergency fund that lets you handle surprises with ease? Is it finally being able to say yes to your dreams? Whatever it is, creating a savings plan is the first step. This book will show you how to set realistic goals, create a budget that works, and stick to it without feeling deprived.

Saving is also about changing the way you think about money. Maybe you've been told that wealth isn't for people like you or that saving is impossible unless you earn six figures. Those ideas couldn't be further from the truth. Saving is for everyone, no matter where you start. Every dollar saved is a step closer to financial independence.

What's Your Why?

Before we move forward, take a moment to think about your why. Why does saving matter to you? Is it about having peace of mind? Giving your children opportunities you didn't have? Retiring comfortably? Whatever your reasons, write them down. Let them remind you of what's possible when you take control of your financial future.

This book is here to guide you, inspire you, and give you the tools you need to make saving a reality. It's not always easy, but it's always worth it. With each chapter, you'll gain more confidence and clarity about how to build the financial future you deserve.

So, are you ready to take that first step? Let's begin.

Chapter 1

Understanding Your Financial Situation

Assessing Your Financial Health

Before you can create a financial plan or start saving effectively, you need to know where you stand. Think of it as taking a snapshot of your financial life. Understanding your income, expenses, debts, and assets gives you a clear picture of what's working, what isn't, and where you can start making changes.

This process might feel intimidating at first, but it's one of the most empowering steps you can take. When you face your finances head-on, you gain control. And when you're in control, you can make decisions that align with your goals and values.

Start with Your Income

Let's begin with the money coming in. Your income is the foundation of your financial health—it dictates how much you can save, spend, and invest. Start by calculating your total monthly income. This includes not just your primary paycheck but also any side hustles, freelance gigs, or other sources of earnings. If your income varies from month to month, take an average of the past three to six months for a more accurate number.

As you look at your income, think about how you feel about it. Is it enough to cover your needs and build toward your goals? If not, consider whether there are opportunities to increase it. Could you negotiate a raise at work? Start a part-time venture? Your income isn't set in stone, and understanding it is the first step toward growth.

Track Your Expenses

Next, it's time to look at where your money goes. Tracking your expenses might sound tedious, but it's an eye-opening exercise that can reveal spending patterns you didn't even realize you had. Start by gathering all your bank statements, credit card bills, and receipts from the past few months. Look at every transaction and group them into categories like housing, transportation, groceries, dining out, entertainment, and subscriptions.

As you review your spending, ask yourself: Are these expenses in line with my priorities? Do I truly value the things I'm spending money on? Often, we find that small, unnecessary expenses—like subscription services we barely use or frequent takeout meals—add up quickly. Identifying these areas gives you the opportunity to redirect that money toward savings or other goals.

If this step feels overwhelming, take it one day at a time. Track your spending daily for a month and see where your money is going. Use a notebook, a spreadsheet, or a budgeting app—whatever works best for you. The goal isn't to judge yourself; it's to understand your habits so you can make intentional choices.

Evaluate Your Debts

Debt can feel like a heavy burden, but understanding it is the key to overcoming it. Start by listing all your debts, including credit cards, student loans, car loans, and any other balances you owe. Write down the total amount owed, the interest rate, and the minimum monthly payment for each.

Once you have this information, think about how your debt fits into your overall financial picture. Are you making progress on paying it down, or does it feel like you're stuck in a cycle of minimum payments? If the latter is true, it might be time to explore strategies like consolidating debt, negotiating lower interest rates, or focusing on high-interest debts first.

But don't let your debt define you. Many people carry debt, and it's possible to manage it while working toward your savings goals. The important thing is to stay proactive and seek solutions rather than letting it overwhelm you.

Take Stock of Your Assets

Now, let's talk about what you own. Your assets include anything of value, like a home, car, savings accounts, retirement accounts, investments, and even valuable possessions. Write down each asset and its estimated value. This might include your current bank balances, the market value of your home, or the resale value of your car.

As you review your assets, ask yourself how they contribute to your financial health. Are they growing in value? Are they aligned with your goals? For example, if you have a retirement account, are you contributing regularly to it? If you own a home, are you building equity? Understanding your assets helps you see the full picture of your financial situation and identify opportunities to grow your wealth.

Create a Financial Snapshot

Once you've assessed your income, expenses, debts, and assets, it's time to put it all together. This financial snapshot shows your net worth—the difference between what you own and what you owe. If your assets exceed your debts, congratulations! You're building wealth. If your debts outweigh your assets, don't worry—this is simply your starting point, not your destination.

To create your financial snapshot, subtract your total debts from your total assets. This number is your net worth. While it might feel disheartening if your net worth is negative, remember that the purpose of this exercise is to give you a baseline. It's not about where you are today; it's about where you're headed.

Reflect and Set Intentions

Now that you have a clear picture of your financial health, take a moment to reflect. How do you feel about what you've discovered? Are there areas where you feel strong and areas where you want to improve? Write down your thoughts. This reflection will help you identify your priorities as you move forward.

Think about what you want to achieve in the next six months, year, or five years. Do you want to pay off a specific debt? Build an emergency fund? Start investing? Use what you've learned about your financial health to set intentions for the future. These intentions will become the foundation for your savings goals and action plans.

Take Small Steps Today

Understanding your financial health is a powerful step, but it's just the beginning. Start small by choosing one area to focus on, whether it's cutting back on unnecessary expenses, creating a plan to tackle debt, or increasing your savings by a small percentage. Remember, progress is made in small, consistent steps.

As you take these steps, remind yourself why this matters. Your financial health isn't just about numbers—it's about freedom, security, and the ability to live life on your terms. By taking control of your finances today, you're building a foundation for a brighter tomorrow.

Common Financial Pitfalls to Avoid

Saving money is one of the most empowering things you can do for yourself and your future, but it's not always easy. Sometimes, the obstacles aren't just external—they're the habits and choices we make without even realizing their impact. Identifying these common financial pitfalls is the first step to overcoming them and making better decisions. When you're aware of what's holding you back, you can take control and start directing your money toward the things that matter most.

Living Beyond Your Means

One of the most common pitfalls is spending more than you earn. It's easy to fall into this trap, especially when credit cards and buy-now-pay-later options make it seem effortless to have what you want right now. Whether it's upgrading to the latest phone, dining out frequently, or shopping for things you don't need, these small choices can quickly add up.

Think about your spending habits. Are there areas where you're overextending yourself? It might feel satisfying in the moment, but over time, living beyond your means creates stress and limits your ability to save. The good news is that it's possible to shift this mindset. Start by asking yourself a simple question before making any purchase: Do I truly need this, or can it wait? This one pause can help you make intentional choices that align with your financial goals.

Emotional Spending

We all have days when emotions—whether it's stress, boredom, or sadness—lead us to spend money as a way to cope. You might treat yourself to an expensive meal after a tough day or buy something online just to feel a momentary spark of happiness. While it's natural to want a little comfort, relying on spending as a solution can sabotage your savings.

If emotional spending resonates with you, take a moment to reflect. When you feel the urge to spend, try redirecting that energy. Instead of clicking "add to cart," could you call a friend, take a walk, or journal your feelings? Recognizing these patterns and finding healthier outlets can help you break free from the cycle of emotional spending.

Ignoring the "Small" Expenses

It's easy to overlook small, everyday expenses because they don't seem significant on their own. A coffee here, a snack there, or a few dollars for a subscription you barely use might not feel like much in the moment. But over time, these small leaks can drain your budget.

Imagine how much you could save if you redirected even a fraction of those small expenses. Start by reviewing your bank statements for recurring charges or frequent purchases. Are there things you could cut back on without sacrificing your quality of life? Maybe it's cancelling a streaming service you no longer watch or making coffee at home a few times a week. These small adjustments can lead to big savings over time.

Relying Too Heavily on Credit Cards

Credit cards can be a helpful tool when used wisely, but relying on them too much can quickly lead to debt. If you're only making minimum payments, carrying a balance month after month, or using credit for non-essential purchases, it's time to reevaluate.

Start by being honest with yourself about how and why you use credit cards. Are they filling gaps in your budget, or are they enabling habits that don't align with your goals? Consider setting a limit on how often you use credit and focus on paying down your existing balances. Every dollar you save in interest is a dollar you can put toward building your future.

Failing to Plan for Irregular Expenses

Unexpected expenses—like car repairs, medical bills, or gifts during the holidays—can wreak havoc on your finances if you're not prepared. Many people fall into the trap of thinking these costs are out of their control, but the truth is, you can plan for them.

Take a moment to think about the expenses that tend to catch you off guard. Could you create a separate savings account for these irregular costs? By setting aside a small amount each month, you'll be ready when the time comes, and you won't have to dip into your emergency fund or go into debt.

Skipping the Budget

Budgeting might sound restrictive, but it's actually one of the most freeing things you can do for your finances. Without a budget, it's easy to lose track of where your money is going and end up wondering why there's nothing left to save.

If you've avoided budgeting in the past, consider reframing how you think about it. A budget isn't about saying no—it's about making room for what matters most. Start by tracking your income and expenses for a month. Look for patterns and identify areas where you can cut back. Even a simple plan, like the 50/30/20 rule, can help you create balance and prioritize saving.

Procrastinating on Saving

"I'll start saving when I make more money." Does this sound familiar? Procrastination is a common pitfall, but the truth is, there's never a "perfect" time to start saving. Waiting only delays the benefits and leaves you less prepared for the future.

Even if your budget feels tight, saving something—anything—is better than nothing. Start small, even if it's just $5 or $10 a week. The act of saving builds a habit, and over time, those small amounts add up. Remember, it's not about how much you save initially; it's about being consistent and making saving a priority.

Falling for Lifestyle Inflation

As your income grows, it's natural to want to improve your lifestyle. Maybe you upgrade your car, move to a bigger apartment, or start dining out more often. While it's okay to enjoy the fruits of your labor, be mindful of lifestyle inflation—the tendency to increase your spending as your income rises.

Instead of letting every raise or bonus slip through your fingers, consider how much of that extra money you could save. Could you commit to putting 50% of any new income toward your goals? By keeping your expenses stable while your income grows, you'll accelerate your savings and build wealth faster.

The Power of Awareness

The most important step in overcoming these pitfalls is awareness. Take some time to reflect on your habits and choices. Which of these pitfalls do you recognize in yourself? Write them down and think about the changes you could make to avoid them. Remember, this isn't about being perfect—it's about making progress and taking small steps in the right direction.

Setting a Baseline for Savings

Determining how much you can start saving isn't about squeezing every penny or depriving yourself of joy; it's about understanding your finances and finding a balance that works for you.

This process is empowering because it puts you in control. No matter your current financial situation, you have the power to start saving and move closer to the future you want.

Why Start Small?

When it comes to saving, many people feel overwhelmed by the idea that they need to put away large amounts right away. This mindset can stop you before you even begin. The reality is that small, consistent steps are often the most effective. Saving just a little today builds the habit and sets the foundation for long-term success.

Think of saving as planting a seed. Even the smallest effort can grow into something significant over time. Starting small also makes saving feel achievable rather than stressful. It's not about waiting until you can save hundreds of dollars each month—it's about starting with whatever amount fits your life right now.

Understanding Your Starting Point

Before you decide how much to save, it's important to understand your financial baseline. This means looking at your income, expenses, and any existing obligations like debt. The goal here isn't to judge yourself or feel discouraged; it's to gain clarity so you can make informed decisions.

Start by calculating your monthly income. Include all sources, such as your paycheck, side gigs, or any other consistent earnings. Once you know how much money is coming in, review your expenses. Look at necessities like rent, utilities, groceries, and transportation, as well as discretionary spending like dining out or entertainment. By comparing your income to your expenses, you'll see how much flexibility you have for saving.

As you do this, ask yourself some key questions: Are there areas where you're overspending? Could you cut back on non-essential items to free up some money for savings? Even small adjustments can make a big difference.

Setting Realistic Goals

Once you have a clear picture of your finances, it's time to set a baseline for savings. The amount you save doesn't need to be perfect or impressive—it just needs to be something you can commit to consistently. Start by choosing a percentage of your income to save each month. For example, if you can save 5% or even 1%, that's a great starting point.

Let's say you earn $3,000 a month, and you decide to save 5%. That's $150. It might not seem like much, but over a year, that adds up to $1,800. The key is consistency. Even saving $20 or $50 a month can build momentum and prove to yourself that saving is possible.

Automating Your Savings

One of the easiest ways to ensure you stick to your savings plan is to automate it. When you set up automatic transfers from your checking account to your savings account, you remove the temptation to spend that money. Treat your savings like any other bill—something you pay regularly without fail.

Many banks and financial apps allow you to set up these automatic transfers, and some even let you round up purchases to the nearest dollar and deposit the difference into your savings. These small, automated actions can have a significant impact over time.

Building an Emergency Fund First

When setting a baseline for savings, it's important to focus on building an emergency fund. This fund is your safety net for unexpected expenses, like car repairs or medical bills. Having an emergency fund can prevent you from going into debt when life throws you a curveball.

Start by deciding how much you'd like your emergency fund to hold. A good initial goal is $500 to $1,000, but eventually, aim for three to six months' worth of living expenses. Begin saving toward this goal with whatever amount you can manage, and watch it grow. Even small contributions can give you peace of mind and financial stability.

Adjusting Your Baseline Over Time

Your baseline for savings isn't set in stone—it can and should evolve as your financial situation changes. Maybe you get a raise at work, pay off a debt, or find ways to cut expenses. When this happens, consider increasing the amount you save. For example, if you start by saving 5% of your income, you might aim for 10% or 15% down the line.

On the flip side, if unexpected circumstances arise—like losing a job or facing a medical expense—it's okay to adjust your savings temporarily. The goal is to make saving a sustainable habit, not a source of stress.

What matters is that you keep the habit alive, even if the amount fluctuates.

Reflecting on Your Motivation

As you work to set your baseline for savings, take a moment to think about your motivation. Why do you want to save? Is it to create financial security, achieve a specific goal, or provide for your family's future? Write down your reasons and keep them somewhere visible. When saving feels challenging, these reminders will help you stay focused and committed.

Celebrating Small Wins

It's easy to get discouraged if you feel like your savings aren't growing quickly enough. But every step forward, no matter how small, is worth celebrating. Did you save $20 this month? That's progress. Did you avoid an unnecessary purchase and put the money into your savings instead? That's a win.

Take pride in the effort you're making. Saving isn't just about the numbers—it's about the mindset and habits you're building. Acknowledge your progress and use it as fuel to keep going.

The Bigger Picture

Setting a baseline for savings isn't just about having money in the bank—it's about creating opportunities and freedom. It's about taking control of your financial future and proving to yourself that you're capable of achieving your goals. Every dollar you save is a step toward the life you deserve.

As you establish your baseline and start saving, remember that this is just the beginning. Your baseline is the foundation for everything else you'll build—whether it's paying off debt, investing, or creating generational wealth. The most important thing is to start today, with whatever you can. Your future self will thank you for it.

You've got this. Keep going, and don't underestimate the power of even the smallest steps. They're leading you toward something incredible.

Chapter 2

Defining Your Savings Goals

Short-Term vs. Long-Term Goals

Understanding the difference between short-term and long-term goals—and how to prioritize them—can help you create a savings plan that's both practical and inspiring. Each type of goal plays an essential role in your financial well-being, and balancing them ensures that your money works for you now and in the future.

What Are Short-Term Goals?

Short-term goals are savings targets you aim to achieve within a few months to a couple of years. These goals often focus on immediate needs, such as paying off small debts, building an emergency fund, or saving for a vacation. They're tangible, often easier to visualize, and can provide quick wins that boost your confidence and momentum.

Think about what short-term goals might matter most to you right now. Is it setting aside money for holiday gifts? Preparing for a friend's wedding? Covering a major purchase like a new appliance? These goals are important because they help you handle life's demands without feeling overwhelmed or resorting to credit card debt.

The beauty of short-term goals is that they allow you to experience the benefits of saving relatively quickly. Each time you accomplish one, you build a sense of pride and proof that saving works. It's not just about the money—it's about the habit, discipline, and freedom that comes with it.

What Are Long-Term Goals?

Long-term goals, on the other hand, are focused on the bigger picture. These are the dreams and plans that take years to achieve, like buying a home, retiring comfortably, or funding your child's education. Long-term goals require patience and commitment because their impact isn't immediate. But they're no less important—in fact, they often represent some of life's most meaningful aspirations.

Long-term savings might feel less urgent than short-term needs, but neglecting them can lead to missed opportunities. For example, starting to save for retirement in your 20s or 30s allows your investments to grow significantly through compound interest. Waiting until your 40s or 50s means you'll need to save much more to reach the same goal.

When you think about your long-term goals, what comes to mind? Maybe it's building generational wealth, owning property, or starting a business that creates financial independence. These dreams can seem far away, but breaking them into smaller, actionable steps makes them achievable.

The Importance of Balancing Both

Life is a mix of immediate demands and long-term aspirations, and your savings plan should reflect that. Focusing solely on short-term goals might leave you unprepared for the future, while only prioritizing long-term goals could leave you scrambling when unexpected expenses arise. The key is to strike a balance that aligns with your values and circumstances.

Start by thinking about your current situation. If you don't have an emergency fund or are struggling with high-interest debt, prioritizing short-term goals makes sense. Once those are under control, you can shift more focus to long-term savings. It's not about choosing one over the other—it's about adjusting the balance as your needs and opportunities evolve.

Setting Priorities That Work for You

So, how do you decide which goals to prioritize? The answer lies in understanding your values and what matters most to you. Take a moment to reflect: What gives you peace of mind? What excites you about the future? These answers will guide you in creating a savings plan that feels purposeful and motivating.

If short-term security is your priority, focus on goals like building an emergency fund or paying off a credit card balance. If you're dreaming about a long-term milestone, like owning a home or starting a retirement account, start allocating a portion of your income toward that goal, even if it's small. The key is to create a plan that reflects your unique situation and aspirations.

Creating a Savings Plan for Both

Balancing short-term and long-term goals doesn't have to be complicated. Begin by allocating a percentage of your income to each. For example, you might dedicate 60% of your savings to short-term goals and 40% to long-term goals. Over time, as short-term needs are met, you can increase the portion allocated to long-term savings.

Think of it this way: Your short-term savings are the stepping stones that keep you stable, while your long-term savings are the foundation for something greater. Both are necessary, and both deserve your attention.

Staying Flexible

One of the most important things to remember about savings goals is that life happens. Your priorities might shift as circumstances change, and that's okay. Flexibility is key to maintaining a savings plan that works for you. If an unexpected expense arises, it's okay to pause long-term savings temporarily to address short-term needs. Similarly, if you receive a bonus or windfall, consider using it to give your long-term goals a boost.

Reflect regularly on your goals and adjust as needed. What felt important a year ago might not be as relevant today, and that's normal. Savings is a dynamic process that evolves with your life.

Reflection: What Matters Most to You?

Take a moment to think about your own goals. Write them down—both short-term and long-term. What do you want to achieve in the next year? What about in the next five, ten, or twenty years? Seeing your goals on paper can make them feel more real and motivate you to take action.

Ask yourself: Which goals feel most urgent right now? Which ones excite you the most about the future? Use your answers to create a savings plan that aligns with your values and vision.

The Bigger Picture

Defining your savings goals isn't just about setting financial targets—it's about creating a life that reflects your dreams and priorities. Short-term and long-term goals work together to give you stability, freedom, and the ability to pursue what matters most. By understanding the difference between them and finding a balance, you're taking a powerful step toward the financial future you deserve.

Remember, every dollar you save brings you closer to your goals, no matter how small. Start today, and trust that the effort you put in now will pay off in ways you can't even imagine.

Creating a Vision for Your Future

When you think about your future, what do you see? Is it a home filled with warmth and security, the thrill of running your own business, or the freedom to explore new places and experiences? Your savings goals aren't just numbers in a bank account—they're the bridge to the life you want to live. Connecting your financial efforts to personal dreams transforms saving from a chore into an exciting, purpose-driven habit. When you have a clear vision of your future, every dollar saved becomes a step toward something meaningful.

Dreams That Inspire Action

The power of a dream lies in its ability to motivate and guide you. But dreams often feel distant or intangible, especially when they're big, like owning a home or starting a business. The first step to turning your dreams into reality is defining them. What excites you about the future? What kind of life do you want to create?

Maybe you've always imagined having a place to call your own—a sanctuary that reflects your style and gives your family stability. Or perhaps you've been thinking about starting a business that not only brings financial independence but also fulfills a passion or fills a gap in your community. Or it could be something as personal as exploring new countries, soaking in different cultures, and broadening your perspective.

Take a moment to picture these dreams. What would achieving them feel like? Let yourself connect emotionally to the possibilities. These aren't just fantasies—they're your why, the reasons you save and make intentional financial choices.

The Importance of Clarity

A vision without clarity is like a destination without a map. To bring your dreams closer, you need to define them in detail. Think about what each dream means to you and what achieving it would require. If owning a home is your goal, what kind of home do you envision? Where would it be located? How much might it cost? If traveling the world excites you, what destinations are at the top of your list? How long would you want to spend exploring, and what would the costs look like?

Clarity turns dreams into actionable goals. Instead of saying, "I want to save for a house," you can aim for, "I want to save $20,000 for a down payment on a three-bedroom home within the next five years." This shift makes your goal tangible and gives you a clear target to work toward.

Aligning Your Goals with Your Values

Your savings goals should reflect what matters most to you. This alignment ensures that every dollar saved feels purposeful. Ask yourself what values drive your vision for the future. Is it security, freedom, family, or creativity? Understanding these core values helps you prioritize your goals and stay motivated.

For example, if family is your top priority, saving for a home where your loved ones can gather might take precedence. If freedom excites you, building a savings cushion that allows you to leave a job and start your own business could be your focus. There's no right or wrong answer—it's about aligning your savings with what truly matters to you.

Breaking Dreams Into Steps

Big dreams can feel overwhelming if you don't know where to start. That's why it's important to break them into smaller, manageable steps. Instead of focusing solely on the end goal, identify the milestones along the way.

Let's say you want to save for an extended vacation to Europe. Start by estimating the total cost, including flights, accommodations, food, and activities. If the trip costs $10,000 and you have two years to save, your monthly savings target would be around $417. Breaking it down like this makes the goal feel more achievable.

Similarly, if your dream is to start a business, think about the upfront costs—equipment, marketing, or certifications. Once you have a clear number, you can set aside a portion of your income each month to build the capital you need.

Overcoming Doubts and Barriers

Sometimes, dreams can feel out of reach, especially when financial barriers or self-doubt come into play. You might think, "I'll never have enough to buy a home," or "Traveling is for people who earn way more than I do." These thoughts can hold you back, but they don't have to define your reality.

Start by challenging these doubts. Instead of focusing on the obstacles, look for solutions. Could you save more by adjusting your budget? Are there resources, like grants or programs, that could help? Remember, every dream starts with a single step, no matter how small. The key is to believe in your ability to make progress.

Visualizing Success

Visualization is a powerful tool for staying motivated. When you can see yourself achieving your goals, it becomes easier to make the sacrifices and choices needed to get there. Spend a few minutes each day picturing your future. Imagine yourself unlocking the door to your first home, hearing the cheers of customers at your grand opening, or stepping off a plane into a new country.

These mental images aren't just wishful thinking—they're reminders of why you're saving. Write down your vision or create a vision board filled with images and words that represent your dreams. Place it somewhere you'll see every day as a source of inspiration.

Staying Flexible

While having a clear vision is important, life doesn't always go as planned. Unexpected expenses, shifts in priorities, or changes in circumstances can impact your savings goals. Flexibility is key to staying on track. If a dream feels temporarily out of reach, it's okay to adjust your timeline or savings amount. What matters is that you keep moving forward, even if progress feels slower than expected.

Reflecting on Your Dreams

As you think about your future, take time to reflect. What are your dreams, and why do they matter to you? How would achieving them impact your life? Write down your thoughts, and let them guide your financial decisions. Connecting your savings to personal dreams gives your efforts meaning and keeps you focused on what truly matters.

Turning Dreams Into Reality

Your future isn't something that just happens—it's something you create. By linking your savings to your personal dreams, you're taking control and building a life that reflects your values and aspirations. Whether it's owning a home, starting a business, or traveling the world, every dollar saved brings you closer to the life you've imagined.

SMART Goals for Savings

Setting savings goals is more than just writing down a wish list—it's about creating a roadmap that guides you to the life you want. The SMART framework helps you do just that by breaking goals into clear, actionable steps. **SMART** goals are **Specific**, **Measurable**, **Achievable**, **Relevant**, and **Time-Bound**. They take your dreams and transform them into plans you can stick to, no matter where you're starting from.

When your savings goals are SMART, you give yourself the tools to stay focused, motivated, and accountable. Let's explore how to apply each part of the SMART framework to your financial goals.

Specific: Define Exactly What You Want

Vague goals often lead to vague results. Saying, "I want to save money" is a good start, but it doesn't give you a clear direction. What are you saving for? How much do you need? When you make your goal specific, it becomes easier to understand and act on.

For example, instead of saying, "I want to save for a vacation," you could say, "I want to save $3,000 for a two-week trip to Italy." This version answers the "what", "why", and "how much" of your goal. It paints a picture of what success looks like and gives you a target to aim for.

Take a moment to think about one of your savings goals. Write it down and ask yourself if it's specific enough. If not, add more detail. The clearer your goal, the more motivated you'll be to work toward it.

Measurable: Track Your Progress

A goal without a way to measure it can leave you feeling lost. How will you know if you're on track or how close you are to achieving your goal? Adding measurable elements allows you to monitor your progress and stay motivated.

Let's use the vacation example. If you need $3,000 and have six months to save, you can break it down into monthly milestones: $500 per month. By tracking your savings each month, you can see how much closer you're getting to your goal.

Consider creating a visual tracker, like a chart or graph, to measure your progress. Every time you save, update it. Seeing your efforts add up can give you a sense of accomplishment and keep you going, even when it feels challenging.

Achievable: Set Goals You Can Reach

Your savings goals should challenge you, but they should also be realistic. Setting a goal that's too ambitious can lead to frustration and burnout, while setting a goal that's too easy might not feel meaningful. The key is to find a balance—stretch yourself, but stay within the realm of possibility.

Think about your current income, expenses, and financial obligations. If saving $500 a month for six months isn't feasible, adjust your timeline or amount. Maybe you save $300 a month for ten months instead. The important thing is to set a goal that feels manageable while still pushing you to grow.

Ask yourself: Is this goal realistic based on my current financial situation? If not, what adjustments can I make to increase my chances of success?

Relevant: Align Your Goals with Your Values

Saving just for the sake of saving can feel unmotivating. Your goals should reflect what truly matters to you, whether that's providing for your family, achieving financial freedom, or pursuing a lifelong dream. When your goals are relevant to your life and values, they feel more meaningful and rewarding.

Take a moment to think about why your savings goal is important. How does it align with your long-term vision? For instance, if your dream is to buy a home, saving for a down payment is relevant because it directly supports that aspiration. Similarly, if you value security, building an emergency fund is a goal that resonates with your priorities.

Connecting your goals to your values not only gives them purpose but also helps you stay committed, even when the road feels tough.

Time-Bound: Set a Deadline

Without a deadline, your goal can feel endless, and procrastination can creep in. Setting a time frame creates urgency and keeps you accountable. It's the difference between saying, "I want to save $5,000 someday" and saying, "I want to save $5,000 in 12 months."

When setting your time frame, consider what's realistic based on your income and expenses. If you have a larger goal, break it into smaller chunks with shorter deadlines. For example, if your goal is to save $20,000 in three years, focus on saving $7,000 in the first year and adjust as needed.

Deadlines create a sense of structure and give you a clear endpoint to work toward. They help you turn a dream into a plan and keep you focused on taking consistent action.

Putting It All Together

Now that you understand each part of the SMART framework, let's see how it works when combined. Imagine you want to save for a car. A SMART goal might look like this:

- **Specific**: "I want to save $10,000 for a used car."
- **Measurable**: "I'll track my progress by saving $500 a month."
- **Achievable**: "Based on my budget, $500 a month is doable."
- **Relevant**: "Having a reliable car will help me get to work and improve my quality of life."
- **Time-Bound**: "I'll achieve this goal within 20 months."

By breaking your goal into these parts, you create a plan that's clear, actionable, and tied to your values. You can see exactly what you need to do and when, making it easier to stay motivated and consistent.

Reflecting on Your Own Goals

Take some time to think about your savings goals. Write them down and apply the SMART framework to each one. Are they specific, measurable, achievable, relevant, and time-bound? If not, revise them until they meet these criteria. This exercise can transform your goals from vague ideas into actionable plans.

As you work on your goals, remember that they're not set in stone. Life happens, and your priorities may shift. The SMART framework is flexible—it helps you adapt while staying focused on what matters most.

The Power of SMART Goals

When you create SMART goals, you're not just saving money—you're building confidence, discipline, and momentum. Every step you take brings you closer to the future you want. Whether it's a new home, a dream vacation, or financial security, your goals are within reach when you approach them with intention and clarity.

Chapter 3

Building a Budget That Works for You

Tracking Your Income and Expenses

Creating a budget that works for you begins with one essential step: understanding your cash flow. Knowing how much money comes in and where it goes is the foundation for taking control of your finances. It might seem tedious at first, but tracking your income and expenses gives you clarity, reveals hidden spending patterns, and empowers you to make intentional financial choices.

When you can see the big picture of your finances, you're better equipped to create a budget that supports your goals without feeling restrictive. Let's explore practical tools and techniques to help you track your income and expenses effectively.

Why Tracking Matters

Think about the last time you were surprised by how quickly your money disappeared. Maybe you reached the end of the month wondering where it all went. This happens to so many people, not because they're irresponsible, but because money tends to slip away unnoticed when it's not being tracked.

Tracking your income and expenses shines a light on those hidden areas. It helps you identify leaks in your budget, like recurring subscriptions you no longer use or impulse purchases that add up over time. Most importantly, it allows you to see the balance—or imbalance—between your earnings and spending.

Starting with Your Income

Your income is the foundation of your financial health. It's not just about how much you earn, but about how you manage what you earn.

Start by calculating your total monthly income, including all sources such as your regular paycheck, freelance work, side hustles, or any other consistent earnings.

If your income varies from month to month, don't worry. Take an average of the past three to six months to get a realistic picture of your earnings. Write down this number or keep it in a dedicated spreadsheet or app. This is the amount you have to work with when building your budget.

Understanding Your Expenses

Now that you know how much money is coming in, it's time to see where it's going. This step involves looking at every expense, from fixed costs like rent or mortgage payments to variable expenses like groceries, dining out, or entertainment. It's important to be honest and thorough—tracking your expenses only works if you include everything.

Start by gathering your bank statements, credit card bills, and receipts from the past three months. Categorize each expense into groups that make sense for your life, such as housing, transportation, food, subscriptions, and leisure activities. This process might take some time, but it's worth it to get a complete picture.

As you go through this step, reflect on how your spending aligns with your priorities. Are there areas where you're spending more than you realized? Are there expenses that don't bring you much value? These insights will help you make informed decisions when building your budget.

Using Technology to Simplify the Process

Tracking your income and expenses doesn't have to be a manual process. There are countless apps and tools designed to make it easier and more convenient. Apps like Mint, YNAB (You Need a Budget), and

EveryDollar can connect to your bank accounts, automatically categorize transactions, and provide visual summaries of your spending.

If you prefer a more hands-on approach, spreadsheets can be a great option. Tools like Google Sheets or Microsoft Excel allow you to customize your tracking system and analyze your spending patterns in detail. You can even use templates specifically designed for budgeting to save time.

Choose the method that works best for you. The most important thing is consistency. Whether you use an app, a spreadsheet, or pen and paper, commit to reviewing your finances regularly—at least once a week.

Identifying Patterns and Trends

Once you've tracked your income and expenses for a month or two, take a step back and look for patterns. Are there certain categories where you consistently overspend? Do you notice spikes in spending around specific times, like weekends or holidays? Recognizing these trends helps you anticipate future expenses and adjust your budget accordingly.

For example, if you see that dining out takes up a significant portion of your budget, you might decide to cook more meals at home. Or if you notice that subscription services are costing more than expected, you could cancel the ones you no longer use. The goal isn't to eliminate all spending—it's to align your spending with your values and goals.

Reflecting on Emotional Spending

Tracking your expenses also gives you insight into the emotions behind your spending. Many of us make purchases based on feelings rather than needs. Maybe you shop online when you're stressed or treat yourself to expensive meals after a tough week. These patterns aren't inherently bad, but they can derail your savings goals if left unchecked.

Take a moment to reflect on how your emotions influence your spending. Are there alternative ways to cope with stress or celebrate achievements that don't involve spending money? Being mindful of these habits allows you to make more intentional choices.

Creating a Cash Flow Statement

A cash flow statement is a simple tool that shows the balance between your income and expenses. To create one, list all your income sources on one side and all your expenses on the other. Subtract your total expenses from your total income to see whether you're operating with a surplus or deficit.

If you have a surplus, that's fantastic—it means you can allocate more toward savings or other financial goals. If you're operating at a deficit, don't panic. Use this information as a starting point to identify areas where you can cut back or increase your income.

Setting Boundaries with Spending

Tracking your income and expenses isn't just about understanding your finances—it's about setting boundaries that help you stay in control. One effective technique is creating spending limits for each category. For instance, you might decide to spend no more than $300 a month on dining out or $50 on entertainment.

These boundaries aren't meant to feel restrictive; they're designed to help you prioritize what matters most. When you stay within your limits, you free up more money for savings and goals that truly bring value to your life.

Staying Consistent

The most important part of tracking your income and expenses is consistency. It's easy to start strong and then let the habit slip, but regular tracking is what leads to long-term success. Make it a weekly ritual to review your finances, update your tracking tool, and reflect on your progress.

Consistency also allows you to adapt to changes in your financial situation. If you get a raise, face an unexpected expense, or adjust your priorities, tracking helps you stay flexible and in control.

Reflect and Act

Take a moment to reflect on your own cash flow. Do you know how much money you're earning and spending each month? If not, what steps can you take to start tracking today? Remember, this isn't about being perfect—it's about gaining clarity and making progress.

The 50/30/20 Rule

Creating a budget can feel overwhelming, especially if you're trying to manage competing priorities like paying bills, saving for the future, and enjoying your life in the present. That's where the 50/30/20 rule comes in—a simple, practical framework that helps you organize your money without overcomplicating the process. By dividing your income into three categories—needs, wants, and savings—you can create a balanced budget that works for your life and your goals.

This rule isn't about restricting you or making you feel guilty about spending. Instead, it's about giving you clarity and control over your finances while still allowing room for the things that bring you joy.

Breaking Down the 50/30/20 Rule

The 50/30/20 rule divides your after-tax income into three main categories:

- **50% for Needs**: These are the essentials you can't live without, like housing, utilities, groceries, transportation, and insurance.
- **30% for Wants**: This category is for non-essential spending that enhances your life, such as dining out, entertainment, hobbies, and shopping.

- **20% for Savings and Debt Repayment**: This portion goes toward building your financial future, including savings, investments, and paying down debt.

This straightforward approach gives you a clear structure for managing your money while leaving enough flexibility to adapt to your unique situation.

Why the 50/30/20 Rule Works

What makes this framework so effective is its simplicity. It takes the guesswork out of budgeting and provides a baseline to help you make financial decisions. Whether you're trying to save for a big goal, reduce debt, or simply gain better control over your money, the 50/30/20 rule offers a roadmap.

It's also adaptable. Not everyone's life fits perfectly into these percentages, and that's okay. The rule is a guideline, not a strict formula. You can adjust it to suit your income, priorities, and financial goals.

Starting with Needs: The Essentials

The first step in applying the 50/30/20 rule is to identify your needs. These are the non-negotiables—expenses you must cover to maintain your basic quality of life. Think about your rent or mortgage, utility bills, groceries, health insurance, transportation costs, and minimum debt payments.

Take a moment to list your essential expenses. Are they currently within 50% of your after-tax income? If not, consider where you might be able to cut back. For example, could you move to a more affordable housing option, reduce your utility usage, or shop for lower insurance premiums?

Understanding your needs isn't just about numbers—it's about making sure the essentials are covered without stretching yourself too thin. When you allocate enough for these expenses, you create a stable foundation for the rest of your budget.

Wants: Finding Balance Without Guilt

One of the best things about the 50/30/20 rule is that it makes room for enjoyment. The 30% allocated to wants is your permission to spend on the things that make life fun and fulfilling. This might include dining out, attending concerts, traveling, or buying that outfit you've been eyeing.

It's important to distinguish between needs and wants. Groceries are a need, but ordering takeout or grabbing a coffee from your favorite café is a want. Transportation to work is a need, but upgrading to a luxury car might fall into the wants category. These distinctions help you prioritize your spending while still allowing room for indulgence.

The key is moderation. Wants are an important part of your budget, but they shouldn't come at the expense of your needs or savings. Reflect on what truly brings you joy and focus your spending on those things, rather than scattering money on purchases that don't align with your values.

Savings and Debt Repayment: Securing Your Future

The final 20% of your budget is dedicated to building your financial future. This includes contributions to savings accounts, retirement funds, and investments, as well as extra payments toward debt. This category is where you set yourself up for long-term stability and security.

If you're just starting to save, focus on building an emergency fund first. Aim for three to six months' worth of living expenses, which can act as a safety net for unexpected events like job loss or medical emergencies. Once your emergency fund is in place, you can direct more of your savings toward other goals, like buying a home, starting a business, or planning for retirement.

For those with debt, this category also includes making extra payments beyond the minimums. Reducing high-interest debt as quickly as possible frees up more of your income for savings and other goals.

Adjusting the Rule to Fit Your Life

The beauty of the 50/30/20 rule is its flexibility. Your financial situation and priorities might not align perfectly with these percentages, and that's okay. For example, if you're focused on aggressively paying off debt, you might allocate 30% or even 40% of your income to savings and debt repayment, temporarily reducing the amount spent on wants.

Similarly, if you live in an area with a high cost of living, your needs might exceed 50% of your income. In that case, you can adjust the other categories to accommodate your circumstances while still striving for balance.

The key is to use the rule as a starting point, not a rigid requirement. Customize it to fit your life and goals, and revisit your budget regularly to make sure it's still working for you.

Putting the 50/30/20 Rule into Practice

Now that you understand the framework, it's time to put it into action. Start by calculating your after-tax income and dividing it into three categories: needs, wants, and savings. Use a budgeting tool, app, or spreadsheet to track your spending and make adjustments as needed.

As you work through this process, reflect on how the 50/30/20 rule can simplify your financial decisions. Does it give you more clarity about where your money is going? Are there areas where you can adjust your spending to better align with your priorities? The goal isn't perfection—it's progress.

Building a Sustainable Habit

Budgeting with the 50/30/20 rule isn't a one-time activity—it's a habit. Commit to reviewing your budget regularly, whether it's monthly, biweekly, or even weekly. Check in with yourself to see how your spending aligns with your categories and make adjustments as needed.

Over time, this habit will become second nature, giving you confidence and control over your finances. You'll feel empowered to make choices that support your goals and values, knowing that you have a plan in place.

Reflecting on Your Journey

As you apply the 50/30/20 rule, take a moment to reflect on what it means for your financial journey. How does this framework help you balance your present needs with your future goals? What changes can you make today to bring your budget closer to these percentages?

Cutting Costs Without Sacrificing Quality of Life

When you approach saving with intention and creativity, you can reduce expenses without feeling like you're missing out. It's about making choices that align with your values and focusing your resources on what truly brings you joy and fulfillment.

Shifting Your Mindset Around Spending

Before you start cutting costs, it's important to reflect on how you view spending. Sometimes, we spend out of habit, convenience, or a desire to keep up with others. But when you shift your mindset to focus on what really matters to you, saving becomes an empowering choice rather than a sacrifice.

Ask yourself: What are the things in my life that genuinely bring me happiness? What expenses feel unnecessary or less meaningful? By answering these questions, you can start identifying areas where you can spend less without losing what you love.

For example, if eating out with friends is something you value, focus on reducing costs in other areas, like subscriptions you no longer use or impulse purchases. Saving isn't about cutting everything—it's about being selective and intentional.

Cooking at Home Without Feeling Deprived

One of the easiest ways to cut costs is by reducing how often you eat out. But this doesn't mean you have to give up good food or the joy of dining. Cooking at home can be just as satisfying when you experiment with new recipes, host dinner parties, or recreate your favorite restaurant meals.

Plan your meals for the week and shop with a list to avoid overspending on groceries. Look for ways to make cooking fun, like involving family or friends, trying themed dinners, or setting up a weekly "chef's challenge" using ingredients you already have at home.

If you love the social aspect of dining out, consider inviting friends over for a potluck or picnic. These alternatives save money while still allowing you to connect with others over great food.

Finding Low-Cost Entertainment

Entertainment is another area where small changes can lead to big savings. Instead of spending money on movie tickets, concerts, or events every weekend, look for free or low-cost alternatives that still bring you joy. Public parks, local festivals, and community events often offer great experiences without a hefty price tag.

Consider rediscovering hobbies that you've set aside, like painting, gardening, or reading. These activities can provide hours of fulfillment at little to no cost. If you're a fan of movies or shows, take advantage of free trials for streaming services or check out DVDs and books from your local library.

Reflect on what truly brings you happiness in your leisure time. You might find that some of the best memories come from experiences that don't require spending a lot of money.

Smart Shopping Strategies

Cutting costs doesn't mean giving up shopping altogether—it's about shopping smarter. Before making any purchase, take a moment to consider whether it's something you truly need or if it's an impulse buy. If you decide it's worth it, look for ways to get the best value.

Compare prices online, wait for sales, or consider buying gently used items instead of brand-new ones. Thrift stores, consignment shops, and online marketplaces can be treasure troves for finding quality items at a fraction of the cost.

For regular expenses, like groceries or household supplies, consider using coupons, cashback apps, or loyalty programs to save even more. Small savings on everyday items can add up over time.

Reducing Utility Costs Without Sacrificing Comfort

Your monthly bills for electricity, water, and heating are often an overlooked opportunity to save. Simple changes in your habits can reduce these costs without making your home feel less comfortable.

Turn off lights and unplug devices when they're not in use, switch to energy-efficient bulbs, and consider using a programmable thermostat to regulate heating and cooling. In the warmer months, rely more on fans and natural ventilation. During colder months, layering clothes and sealing drafts can help reduce heating expenses.

Reflect on your daily routines and look for small changes that make a difference. These adjustments not only save money but also contribute to a more sustainable lifestyle.

Cutting Down on Subscriptions and Memberships

It's easy to lose track of subscriptions and memberships you're no longer using. Take a close look at your monthly bills and identify any services you could cancel or pause. Whether it's a streaming platform you rarely watch or a gym membership you haven't used in months, these recurring charges can add up quickly.

Instead of paying for multiple subscriptions, prioritize the ones you use most. For example, if you enjoy watching TV, choose one streaming service and pause the others until you've watched everything you're interested in. Many platforms allow you to cancel and restart without penalties.

Reflect on which subscriptions truly enhance your life and let go of the ones that don't. Cutting back in this area can free up funds for other priorities.

Embracing Second-hand and DIY Solutions

You don't always have to buy new to enjoy quality and style. Embracing second-hand items or taking on DIY projects can save money while adding a personal touch to your life. Thrift stores, online marketplaces, and community "buy nothing" groups are great places to find furniture, clothing, and household items at low or no cost.

For DIY enthusiasts, consider making gifts, decor, or repairs yourself. Not only does this save money, but it also gives you a sense of accomplishment and creativity. Reflect on what you can reuse or repurpose in your home to reduce expenses while still achieving the results you want.

Practicing Gratitude and Contentment

One of the most powerful ways to cut costs is to focus on what you already have. Practicing gratitude for the things you own and the experiences you enjoy can reduce the urge to constantly buy more. Reflect on the blessings in your life and the memories tied to the things you already have.

When you feel tempted to spend, take a moment to ask yourself if the purchase aligns with your values and goals. Often, simply pausing to reflect can help you make more intentional choices.

Reflecting on Your Priorities

As you explore ways to cut costs, take time to reflect on your priorities and values. What expenses bring you the most joy and fulfillment? What areas feel less meaningful? Use these insights to guide your decisions and focus your resources where they matter most.

Cutting costs doesn't have to feel restrictive. When done with intention, it can create space for the things that truly bring happiness and align with your financial goals.

Chapter 4

Saving on a Tight Budget

Small Steps That Make a Big Difference

You don't need a large income or major sacrifices to start building your savings. Simple, consistent habits can help you create financial stability and move closer to your goals. The key is to focus on actions that fit seamlessly into your life while making a big impact over time.

Automating Your Savings: Set It and Forget It

One of the most effective ways to save is to automate the process. When you set up automatic transfers from your checking account to your savings account, you remove the need to rely on willpower or remember to save each month. It happens in the background, effortlessly.

Think of automating your savings as paying yourself first. Before you even have the chance to spend your income, a portion goes directly into your savings. This habit ensures that saving becomes a priority rather than an afterthought.

Start small, even if it's just $10 or $20 each paycheck. Over time, as your financial situation improves, you can increase the amount. What matters is consistency. These small, automated deposits will grow steadily, and you'll hardly notice the money leaving your account.

Rounding Up Purchases: The Power of Spare Change

Another easy way to save without feeling the pinch is to round up your purchases. Many banks and apps offer programs that round your transactions to the nearest dollar and deposit the difference into your savings account. For example, if you spend $3.75 on coffee, 25 cents would automatically go into savings.

These small amounts might not seem like much, but they add up quickly. Imagine making ten purchases a week, with an average roundup of 50 cents each. That's $5 a week, $20 a month, and $240 a year—all from spare change.

This method works because it's virtually painless. You don't have to think about it or change your spending habits, yet you're consistently saving. It's a reminder that every little bit counts and that even small efforts can have a big impact over time.

Starting a Change Jar: Old School, Still Effective

If you prefer a more tangible approach, consider starting a change jar. At the end of each day, empty your pockets or purse and drop your loose coins into the jar. It might feel like a small act, but watching the jar fill up can be incredibly motivating.

Once the jar is full, deposit the money into your savings account. This habit not only helps you save but also encourages mindfulness about your spending. Over time, you might be surprised at how much you've saved through such a simple practice.

Setting Up Micro-Saving Goals

Breaking down your savings into smaller, short-term goals can make the process feel more manageable and rewarding. Instead of focusing on saving $1,000, set a goal to save $50 this month or $10 this week. These micro-goals keep you motivated and allow you to celebrate small wins along the way.

For example, you could challenge yourself to save $1 a day for a month. By the end of 30 days, you'll have $30—money you might not have saved otherwise. These small amounts are stepping stones to larger financial goals.

Using Cashback and Rewards Wisely

If you use a credit or debit card, take advantage of cashback and rewards programs to stretch your money further. Many cards offer cashback on everyday purchases like groceries, gas, or dining. Use these rewards strategically by depositing the cashback you earn into your savings account.

The same goes for loyalty programs or apps that offer discounts or points. For instance, if you shop at a store with a rewards program, redeem the points for items you need and redirect the money you save into your savings account.

These strategies allow you to make the most of your spending while contributing to your savings without additional effort.

Keeping Track of "Found Money"

Sometimes, money comes into your life unexpectedly—a tax refund, a gift, or even a small bonus at work. Instead of spending it all, commit to saving a portion. This "found money" can give your savings a boost without impacting your regular budget.

Set a rule for yourself, like saving 50% of any unexpected windfall. If you receive a $200 tax refund, for example, you could save $100 and still have $100 to enjoy. This approach allows you to celebrate small financial wins while staying committed to your savings goals.

Reflecting on Your Progress

As you incorporate these small steps into your life, take time to reflect on the progress you're making. How do these habits make you feel about your financial situation? Do you notice a growing sense of control and empowerment? Celebrate every dollar saved, no matter how small, and remind yourself that each step is bringing you closer to your goals.

Leveraging Community Resources

When you're saving on a tight budget, finding support can make all the difference. The good news is that you don't have to do it alone. There are countless programs, grants, and opportunities designed to help you make the most of your resources. As a Black woman, you have access to community-driven initiatives, organizations, and networks that are here to support your financial goals. Leveraging these resources isn't just practical—it's empowering. It's a way of reclaiming your power and building a foundation for a brighter future.

Understanding the Power of Community Support

Community resources exist because we're stronger together. They're designed to lift up individuals and families, helping you access tools and opportunities that might otherwise feel out of reach. Whether it's grants for education, assistance programs for housing, or networking opportunities for entrepreneurs, these resources are here to support you.

Take a moment to think about what you need most right now. Is it help covering basic expenses? Opportunities to advance your career? Support for starting a business? Identifying your priorities will help you focus your energy on the resources that align with your goals.

Financial Assistance Programs

Many local and national programs offer financial assistance to help individuals and families manage their expenses. These programs can provide relief for housing costs, utility bills, or groceries, freeing up more of your income for savings.

For example, organizations like the National Urban League offer financial empowerment programs tailored to Black communities. Similarly, local nonprofits and community centers often have partnerships with food banks, energy assistance programs, and other services designed to ease financial stress. Reaching out to these organizations can open the door to resources you might not even know existed.

Grants and Scholarships for Education

If education is one of your priorities, there are numerous grants and scholarships specifically for Black women. These opportunities can help you pursue degrees, certifications, or skills training without the burden of significant debt.

Organizations like the United Negro College Fund (UNCF) and the Thurgood Marshall College Fund provide scholarships to Black students pursuing higher education. Additionally, groups like the National Black MBA Association offer financial support for advanced business degrees.

Take time to research scholarships and grants in your field of interest. Many organizations prioritize candidates who demonstrate leadership, community involvement, or a commitment to personal growth. Applying might take effort, but the rewards can be life-changing.

Business Grants and Support for Entrepreneurs

If you're dreaming of starting or growing your own business, there are grants and resources tailored specifically for Black women entrepreneurs. These programs recognize the challenges you may face in accessing traditional funding and are here to level the playing field.

The Fearless Fund, for instance, is dedicated to supporting Black women-owned businesses through grants and mentorship. Similarly, organizations like Black Girl Ventures provide funding and resources to help women launch and scale their businesses.

Beyond financial support, these programs often offer networking opportunities, mentorship, and training. By connecting with these communities, you gain not only funding but also valuable guidance and encouragement.

Career Development Resources

Advancing in your career is another powerful way to increase your earning potential and financial stability. Many organizations offer resources to help you build skills, connect with mentors, and find new opportunities.

For example, groups like the National Coalition of 100 Black Women provide leadership development programs and career workshops. Professional associations in your industry may also have networking events, training sessions, and job boards tailored to your field.

Reflect on your career goals and think about the skills or connections you need to reach them. By tapping into these resources, you can position yourself for success and growth.

Leveraging Local Resources

While national organizations play a vital role, don't overlook the resources available in your own community. Local nonprofits, community centers, and churches often offer programs designed to support individuals and families. These might include free financial literacy classes, job placement services, or small business incubators.

Visiting your local library is another great way to access free or low-cost resources. Many libraries offer workshops, career counselling, and even access to grant databases. They're often connected to other community organizations, making them a valuable hub for information.

Building a Support Network

In addition to formal programs, one of the most powerful resources you can leverage is your own network. Friends, family, colleagues, and mentors can provide support, encouragement, and connections to opportunities you might not have discovered on your own.

If you're not sure where to start, consider joining groups or organizations that align with your interests or goals. For example, professional associations, women's groups, or local meetups can introduce you to like-minded individuals who share your aspirations. Building relationships within these communities can lead to collaborations, advice, and new opportunities.

Mindset Shifts for Frugal Living

Living frugally isn't about deprivation or giving up everything you enjoy. It's about making intentional choices with your money and aligning your spending with what truly matters to you. To embrace frugal living, one of the most important steps is redefining the difference between "needs" and "wants." This shift in mindset can transform the way you approach your finances, helping you spend less without sacrificing the quality of your life.

Understanding Needs Versus Wants

Needs are the essentials—things you require to live and maintain a basic quality of life. This includes housing, utilities, groceries, transportation, and healthcare. Wants, on the other hand, are the extras—the things that enhance your life but aren't necessary for survival. These might include dining out, entertainment, luxury items, and vacations.

The challenge is that the line between needs and wants isn't always clear. For example, food is a need but buying takeout every night falls into the category of a want. Transportation is a need, but upgrading to a new car every few years might be more of a want.

To redefine your needs and wants, reflect on each expense in your life and ask yourself a few key questions: Does this expense fulfil a basic necessity? Does it align with my values and priorities? Would I still consider it essential if I were in a financial emergency? These questions can help you gain clarity and make more intentional choices.

Prioritizing What Truly Matters

Once you've identified your needs, it's time to focus on what truly matters in the "wants" category. Wants aren't inherently bad—in fact, they're an important part of a balanced and fulfilling life. The key is to prioritize the ones that bring you the most joy and value.

Think about the last few purchases you made. Which ones left you feeling happy and satisfied? Which ones felt impulsive or unnecessary in hindsight? By reflecting on your spending habits, you can start directing your money toward the things that bring lasting fulfilment and letting go of the expenses that don't.

For example, if travel is something you deeply value, you might decide to allocate more of your discretionary spending toward saving for trips. On the other hand, if you rarely use a gym membership, it might be time to cancel it and redirect that money elsewhere. The goal is to align your spending with your values so that every dollar feels purposeful.

Embracing Intentional Spending

Intentional spending is about making deliberate choices with your money rather than spending out of habit or impulse. It means taking the time to think about your purchases, consider their impact, and decide whether they align with your goals and values.

Before making any purchase, pause and ask yourself a few questions: Do I truly need this? Will it bring value to my life? Is there a more affordable or creative way to achieve the same result? This moment of reflection can help you avoid unnecessary expenses and focus on what really matters.

For example, instead of buying a new outfit for every special occasion, you could shop your own closet or borrow from a friend. Instead of dining out several times a week, you could save those meals for special occasions and cook at home more often. These small shifts might seem minor, but they add up over time, creating more room in your budget for savings and priorities.

Shifting Away from Consumerism

Our culture often encourages constant consumption, sending the message that buying more will make us happier or more successful. But true happiness doesn't come from things—it comes from experiences, relationships, and a sense of purpose. Shifting away from a consumer mindset allows you to focus on what really brings joy and fulfillment.

One way to break free from consumerism is to practice gratitude for what you already have. Take stock of the items, experiences, and people that enrich your life. When you feel tempted to buy something new, pause and reflect on whether it's truly necessary or if it's filling a temporary emotional need. This practice not only saves money but also helps you feel more content and grounded.

Redefining Luxury

Living frugally doesn't mean you have to give up luxury—it means redefining what luxury looks like to you. True luxury isn't always about expensive items or lavish experiences. It can be as simple as enjoying a quiet morning with a cup of coffee, spending quality time with loved ones, or indulging in a creative hobby.

Think about what luxury means to you and how you can incorporate it into your life without overspending. For example, instead of splurging on an expensive spa day, you could create a relaxing self-care routine at home with candles, music, and a long bath. By redefining luxury, you can still enjoy a rich and fulfilling life while staying within your means.

Building a Frugal Mindset

Frugal living is as much about mindset as it is about action. It's about focusing on abundance rather than scarcity and recognizing that you have the power to make choices that align with your values. Instead of feeling restricted by your budget, view it as a tool for creating the life you want.

Celebrate the progress you're making, no matter how small. Each time you save money or make an intentional choice, you're taking a step toward financial freedom. Reflect on how these changes make you feel and the impact they're having on your overall well-being. Frugal living isn't about sacrifice—it's about empowerment and intentionality.

Reflecting on Your Values

As you embrace frugal living, take time to reflect on your values and priorities. What matters most to you? How can you align your spending with those values? By focusing on what truly brings you joy and fulfillment, you can create a life that feels rich and meaningful—without overspending.

Chapter 5

Creating an Emergency Fund

Why Emergency Funds Are Essential

Life has a way of surprising us. Sometimes those surprises are joyful—like a new opportunity or a chance to celebrate—but other times, they bring unexpected challenges. Whether it's a sudden car repair, an unplanned medical expense, or a temporary loss of income, financial emergencies can happen to anyone. What sets financially stable people apart is their preparation. That's where an emergency fund comes in.

An emergency fund is your safety net, your financial cushion that allows you to handle life's surprises without falling into debt or compromising your goals. It's not just about having money in the bank; it's about the peace of mind and confidence that comes from knowing you're ready for whatever comes your way.

A Foundation of Stability

Think about the last time you faced an unexpected expense. Maybe your car broke down, or you had a medical bill that wasn't covered by insurance. How did it feel? For many people, these moments bring stress, worry, and a sense of being unprepared. But with an emergency fund, those feelings shift. Instead of panic, you have a plan. Instead of scrambling to find the money, you know exactly where it will come from.

An emergency fund provides stability. It keeps you grounded when life feels uncertain and gives you the ability to handle challenges without relying on credit cards, loans, or borrowing from friends and family. This stability isn't just financial—it's emotional. Knowing you have a safety net allows you to face emergencies with confidence and clarity.

Protecting Your Long-Term Goals

Without an emergency fund, unexpected expenses can derail your financial progress. Imagine you're saving for a house, building your retirement fund, or working to pay off debt. Suddenly, an emergency arises, and you're forced to dip into your savings or stop making progress on your goals. It's frustrating, disheartening, and can feel like taking two steps back after every step forward.

An emergency fund acts as a buffer. It protects your long-term goals by providing a separate pool of money specifically for unexpected expenses. Instead of pulling from your savings or derailing your progress, you can handle the emergency and stay on track. This separation is essential for building financial security and maintaining momentum toward your dreams.

Reducing Stress and Anxiety

Financial stress is one of the most common sources of anxiety. When you're living paycheck to paycheck or constantly worrying about how you'll cover an unexpected expense, it's hard to focus on anything else. This stress can impact your relationships, your health, and even your ability to perform at work.

An emergency fund reduces this stress. It's a financial cushion, but it's also a mental and emotional one. Knowing you have money set aside for emergencies allows you to approach life with more confidence and less worry. You can focus on your goals, your loved ones, and your well-being instead of constantly thinking about what might go wrong.

Gaining Financial Independence

One of the most empowering aspects of an emergency fund is the sense of independence it provides. When you have money set aside for the unexpected, you're less reliant on others to bail you out in tough times. You don't have to borrow from friends or family, take out high-interest loans, or make financial decisions out of desperation.

This independence isn't just practical—it's deeply empowering. It reinforces the idea that you're in control of your finances and your future. It's a reminder of your strength and resilience, even in the face of challenges.

Building Confidence in Your Financial Journey

Starting an emergency fund can feel daunting, especially if your budget is already tight. But every dollar you save is a step toward greater confidence and security. Even a small emergency fund can make a big difference. For example, having just $500 set aside can cover many common emergencies, like a car repair or an unexpected bill.

As your fund grows, so does your confidence. Each time you add to your emergency fund, you're reinforcing your ability to handle life's challenges. It's a tangible reminder of your progress and your commitment to building a stable, secure future.

Reflecting on Your "Why"

Take a moment to reflect on why an emergency fund matters to you. Is it about reducing stress? Protecting your family? Staying on track with your financial goals? Write down your reasons and keep them somewhere visible. When saving feels challenging, these reminders will keep you motivated and focused.

How Much Should You Save?

When it comes to creating an emergency fund, one of the most common questions is, "How much is enough?" The answer depends on your unique circumstances—your income, expenses, and the life you lead. The right amount for you will look different from someone else's, and that's okay. What matters is figuring out what makes sense for your situation and starting to build your safety net, one step at a time.

Understanding the Basics

At its core, an emergency fund is about preparation. It's money set aside to handle unexpected expenses, like medical bills, car repairs, or even a sudden job loss. The goal is to cover these costs without resorting to debt or sacrificing your financial progress. To achieve this, the amount you save should align with your lifestyle, monthly obligations, and the level of security you want to feel.

For many, the general recommendation is to save three to six months' worth of living expenses. But this range isn't a one-size-fits-all solution. Your ideal amount might be smaller or larger, depending on factors like your job stability, family size, and personal comfort level.

Calculating Your Monthly Expenses

To determine how much you should save, start by calculating your monthly expenses. This includes everything you need to cover your basic needs, such as:

- Housing costs (rent or mortgage)
- Utilities (electricity, water, internet)
- Groceries and household essentials
- Transportation (gas, car payments, public transit)
- Insurance (health, auto, renters)
- Minimum debt payments

Look back at your bank statements and bills from the past few months to get an accurate picture of your spending. Be honest with yourself about what's truly essential and what could be adjusted in an emergency.

Once you have your monthly expenses, you can multiply that number by the number of months you want your emergency fund to cover. For example, if your basic expenses are $2,000 per month and you want a three-month fund, your target would be $6,000.

Considering Your Job Stability

Your job stability plays a significant role in determining how much you should save. If you have a steady job with reliable income, three months of expenses might be enough to feel secure. However, if your income is variable—such as freelance or commission-based work—or if your industry is prone to layoffs, you might want to aim for six months or more.

Think about your own situation. How stable is your income? How long would it likely take you to find a new job if needed? Reflecting on these questions can help you decide how much of a cushion you need to feel safe.

Accounting for Family and Dependents

If you're supporting a family, your emergency fund should account for their needs as well as your own. This might include additional costs like childcare, school supplies, or medical expenses. The more dependents you have, the larger your fund may need to be to provide peace of mind.

Take some time to think about what your family would need in an emergency. Would you need to maintain your current living arrangements, or could you temporarily cut back on certain expenses? These considerations will help you set a realistic goal.

Factoring in Health and Lifestyle

Your health and lifestyle choices can also impact how much you should save. If you have ongoing medical needs or a high-deductible health insurance plan, you might need a larger emergency fund to cover unexpected healthcare costs. Similarly, if your lifestyle involves significant travel or other variable expenses, it's wise to build a bigger cushion.

Reflect on your own health and lifestyle. What kinds of emergencies are most likely to arise for you? Preparing for these possibilities ensures that your fund is tailored to your unique situation.

Starting Small and Growing Over Time

If the idea of saving several months' worth of expenses feels overwhelming, remember that you don't have to do it all at once. Start small, with a goal that feels achievable. Even $500 or $1,000 can make a big difference in your ability to handle minor emergencies.

Once you reach your initial goal, you can continue building your fund gradually. For example, you might aim to save one month's expenses within the next six months, then add another month's worth over the following year. Breaking your goal into smaller milestones makes it more manageable and keeps you motivated.

Adjusting Your Goal as Life Changes

Your emergency fund isn't a set-it-and-forget-it kind of thing. As your life evolves, so should your savings. Major life events—like getting married, having children, or moving to a new city—can change your financial needs and the amount you should have saved.

Make it a habit to revisit your emergency fund annually or whenever your circumstances change. Reflect on whether your current goal still meets your needs or if it's time to adjust. Staying flexible ensures that your fund continues to provide the security you need.

Building Your Fund Gradually

Creating an emergency fund doesn't happen overnight. It's a process that requires consistency, patience, and a few smart strategies to help you stay on track. The good news is that by focusing on small, sustainable steps, you can steadily grow your fund without feeling overwhelmed or sacrificing too much in your day-to-day life. It's not about perfection—it's about progress.

Starting Where You Are

The most important part of building an emergency fund is simply starting. Whether you're setting aside $10 a week or $100 a month, every contribution adds up over time. It's easy to feel discouraged if your savings seem small at first, but remember that consistency is more powerful than the amount itself. Each deposit, no matter how modest, brings you closer to your goal.

Begin by looking at your budget to see what's feasible. If you're not sure where to find extra money to save, start by tracking your expenses and identifying small areas where you can cut back. Maybe it's brewing coffee at home instead of buying it out or pausing a subscription you rarely use. These small adjustments can free up funds that you can redirect toward your emergency fund.

Automating Your Savings

One of the most effective ways to save consistently is to automate the process. When you set up automatic transfers from your checking account to your savings account, you remove the temptation to spend that money and make saving a habit. It's a "set it and forget it" approach that ensures you're making progress without needing to think about it.

If your income is consistent, consider setting up a fixed amount to transfer after each paycheck. Even if it's just $20 or $50, those regular contributions will grow over time. If your income fluctuates, you can adjust the amount month to month, but the key is to stay consistent.

Using Windfalls Wisely

Unexpected windfalls, like tax refunds, bonuses, or gifts, are an excellent opportunity to boost your emergency fund. While it's tempting to spend these extra funds on something fun, consider directing at least a portion of them into savings. You don't have to put it all toward your fund—splitting the money between savings and discretionary spending allows you to enjoy a treat while still making progress on your goals.

Think back to the last time you received a windfall. Did you spend it all, or were you able to save some? Reflecting on how you've handled these opportunities in the past can help you make more intentional choices moving forward.

Building Momentum with Micro-Savings

Sometimes, smaller, more frequent contributions can feel more achievable than larger, infrequent ones. This is where micro-savings strategies come in. Apps and programs that round up your purchases to the nearest dollar and deposit the difference into your savings account are a great example. Over time, these small amounts add up without requiring much effort.

You can also challenge yourself to save in creative ways. For instance, every time you skip a takeout meal or avoid an impulse purchase, transfer the amount you would have spent into your emergency fund. These small wins reinforce the habit of saving and keep you motivated.

Making Saving a Priority

Building your emergency fund requires shifting your mindset to prioritize saving. Instead of viewing it as something you'll do "if there's money left over," treat it as a non-negotiable part of your budget—just like paying your rent or utility bills. By paying yourself first, you ensure that saving remains a priority, even when other expenses arise.

This shift in perspective can be empowering. It's a way of saying, "My future is important, and I'm committed to taking care of myself." Reflect on what this mindset means to you and how it aligns with your values and goals.

Tracking Your Progress

As your emergency fund grows, take time to celebrate your progress. Seeing the balance in your savings account increase is a tangible reminder of your efforts and dedication. Consider keeping a visual tracker, like a chart or graph, to mark each milestone along the way. Whether it's reaching $500, $1,000, or your ultimate goal, these achievements deserve to be acknowledged.

Reflect on how it feels to watch your fund grow. Does it give you a sense of security and confidence? Does it motivate you to keep going? Use these feelings as fuel to stay consistent and committed.

Staying Flexible

Life is unpredictable, and there may be times when you need to adjust your savings plan. Perhaps an unexpected expense arises, or your income changes temporarily. It's okay to scale back your contributions or pause them if needed. What matters is that you don't lose sight of your goal.

When circumstances improve, return to your plan and pick up where you left off. Remember, building an emergency fund is a long-term effort, and progress isn't always linear. Be kind to yourself and stay focused on the bigger picture.

Reflecting on Your Why

Throughout this process, it's important to stay connected to your "why." Why is building an emergency fund important to you? Is it about reducing stress, protecting your family, or staying on track with your financial goals? Write down your reasons and revisit them whenever saving feels challenging.

Your emergency fund is more than just money in the bank—it's a symbol of your resilience, determination, and commitment to your future. By taking consistent steps to build it, you're creating a safety net that will serve you well in both expected and unexpected moments.

Building Habits for a Lifetime

The habits you develop while building your emergency fund can have a lasting impact on your financial journey. As you practice consistency, prioritize saving, and celebrate progress, you're strengthening skills that will benefit you for years to come. These habits can extend beyond your emergency fund, helping you achieve other goals like retirement savings, debt repayment, or investing.

Reflect on the habits you've built so far and the lessons they've taught you. What have you learned about your ability to save? How has this process changed your perspective on money? Use these insights to guide your future financial decisions and continue building a life of stability and security.

Chapter 6

Understanding Savings Accounts and Investment Options

Different Types of Savings Accounts

Savings accounts aren't just about stashing cash; they're about giving your money a safe place to grow while keeping it accessible when you need it. The type of savings account you choose can make a big difference in how your money works for you. Whether you're just starting out or looking to maximize your savings, understanding your options—like high-yield accounts, money market accounts, and certificates of deposit (CDs)—can help you make the best choice for your goals.

High-Yield Savings Accounts: Maximizing Your Interest

High-yield savings accounts are a popular choice for people who want their money to grow faster than it would in a traditional savings account. These accounts offer higher interest rates, meaning you earn more on your balance without any extra effort. While traditional savings accounts often provide minimal interest—sometimes less than 0.1%—high-yield savings accounts can offer rates that are 10 to 20 times higher.

Think of a high-yield account as a simple way to make your money work a little harder. It's especially useful for short-term savings goals, like building an emergency fund or saving for a vacation, because it keeps your money safe and accessible while earning you a better return.

Most high-yield savings accounts are offered by online banks, which can afford to pay higher rates because they have lower overhead costs than traditional brick-and-mortar banks. To get started, look for an account with no monthly fees, a low minimum balance requirement, and a competitive interest rate.

Reflect on how much more motivated you'd feel to save if your money was growing faster. A high-yield savings account can provide that extra push to keep you consistent and committed.

Money Market Accounts: A Flexible Option for Savers

Money market accounts are another great option for savers, offering a mix of features from both savings and checking accounts. Like high-yield savings accounts, they typically pay higher interest rates than traditional savings accounts. But what sets money market accounts apart is their added flexibility.

With a money market account, you often have the ability to write checks or use a debit card for withdrawals—something you don't usually get with a standard savings account. This makes money market accounts a good choice if you want to earn interest while keeping some accessibility for occasional transactions.

However, it's important to know that money market accounts often come with higher minimum balance requirements than regular savings accounts. If your balance falls below the required minimum, you might face fees or a lower interest rate.

Consider whether you need the flexibility of check-writing or debit card access. If you do, a money market account might be the right fit for your goals. It offers the perfect balance of earning potential and convenience.

Certificates of Deposit (CDs): Locking in Higher Returns

Certificates of deposit, or CDs, are a savings tool designed for people who can commit to leaving their money untouched for a set period. In exchange for this commitment, banks typically offer higher interest rates than you'd get with a savings or money market account. The longer the term of the CD, the higher the interest rate you're likely to earn.

CDs are ideal for goals with a specific timeline. For example, if you're saving for a down payment on a house in three years, a three-year CD could be a great way to earn more interest while keeping your money safe. Just be sure you're comfortable locking your funds away, as withdrawing from a CD before its maturity date often results in penalties.

Reflect on your financial goals and the timelines associated with them. If you have a clear plan and don't need immediate access to your funds, a CD can be a powerful way to grow your savings. It's a tool that rewards patience and planning.

Balancing Access and Growth

Each type of savings account offers unique benefits, and the right one for you depends on your priorities. High-yield savings accounts are great for flexibility and consistent growth, money market accounts add an extra layer of convenience, and CDs provide higher returns for those willing to lock in their funds.

Think about what matters most to you. Do you need immediate access to your money, or are you willing to trade some accessibility for higher returns? Reflecting on your financial needs and goals will help you choose the account that aligns best with your situation.

Using Multiple Accounts for Different Goals

You don't have to limit yourself to just one type of account. Many people find it helpful to use multiple accounts for different purposes. For example, you might keep your emergency fund in a high-yield savings account for easy access, use a money market account for medium-term goals, and invest in CDs for long-term savings.

This approach allows you to take advantage of the strengths of each account type while tailoring your savings strategy to your unique needs.

Reflect on your own goals and consider how different accounts could help you achieve them more effectively.

Protecting Your Money

One of the most important benefits of these savings accounts is their safety. All the account types mentioned—high-yield savings accounts, money market accounts, and CDs—are typically insured by the Federal Deposit Insurance Corporation (FDIC) up to $250,000 per depositor, per bank. This means your money is protected even if the bank experiences financial trouble.

Knowing that your savings are secure provides peace of mind and allows you to focus on growing your funds without worry. It's one of the reasons these accounts are such a reliable choice for building financial stability.

Reflecting on Your Savings Strategy

As you consider your options, take a moment to reflect on your current savings habits. Are you using an account that maximizes your earnings and aligns with your goals? If not, what steps can you take to explore better options?

The Role of Investments in Saving

Investments offer the opportunity to build wealth beyond what a standard savings account can provide, helping you achieve long-term goals like retirement, buying a home, or funding your children's education. By understanding the basics of investment vehicles like stocks, bonds, mutual funds, and more, you can start making informed decisions that align with your financial future.

What Makes Investments Different from Savings?

The primary difference between savings and investments is the level of risk and reward. A savings account keeps your money safe and accessible while earning modest interest. Investments, on the other hand, involve putting your money into assets that have the potential to grow over time but also carry some level of risk.

Investing isn't about gambling or trying to "strike it rich" overnight. It's a calculated way to grow your wealth over the long term. By choosing the right investments and allowing them time to grow, you can achieve returns that far outpace traditional savings methods.

Understanding Stocks: Owning a Piece of a Company

Stocks, also known as equities, represent ownership in a company. When you buy a stock, you're purchasing a small piece of that company, and your returns come from two main sources: dividends (a share of the company's profits) and capital gains (the increase in the stock's value over time).

Stocks are often considered one of the most effective ways to build wealth because they tend to provide higher returns than other investment vehicles over the long term. However, they also come with greater risks, as stock prices can fluctuate significantly in the short term.

If you're new to investing, start by researching companies or industries you're familiar with. Reflect on your comfort level with risk and consider investing in stable, well-established companies if you're looking for a less volatile option. Alternatively, you can explore index funds or exchange-traded funds (ETFs), which are collections of stocks designed to mirror the performance of a specific market index.

Bonds: A More Stable Option

Bonds are often referred to as fixed-income investments because they provide regular interest payments over a set period. When you buy a bond, you're essentially lending money to a government or corporation in exchange for periodic interest payments and the return of your principal at the end of the bond's term.

Bonds are generally considered safer than stocks, making them a good option for conservative investors or those nearing retirement. However, their returns tend to be lower than those of stocks. The key is finding the right balance between risk and reward based on your financial goals and timeline.

Think of bonds as a way to add stability to your investment portfolio. Reflect on whether a mix of bonds and stocks could help you achieve your goals while managing risk effectively.

Mutual Funds: Diversification Made Easy

Mutual funds pool money from multiple investors to buy a diversified portfolio of stocks, bonds, or other assets. They're managed by professional fund managers who make investment decisions on your behalf. This makes mutual funds an excellent option for beginners or those who prefer a hands-off approach.

One of the biggest advantages of mutual funds is diversification. By spreading your money across multiple investments, you reduce the risk of losing everything if one particular asset performs poorly. However, mutual funds come with fees, so it's important to choose funds with low expense ratios to maximize your returns.

Reflect on how much time and effort you're willing to dedicate to managing your investments. If you'd rather let a professional handle the details, a mutual fund might be the perfect choice.

ETFs: A Modern Twist on Mutual Funds

Exchange-traded funds (ETFs) are similar to mutual funds but trade like stocks on an exchange. This means you can buy and sell them throughout the day, just like individual stocks. ETFs are known for their low fees and flexibility, making them a popular choice for investors of all levels.

ETFs often track specific indexes, sectors, or themes, allowing you to tailor your investments to your interests and goals. For example, you could invest in an ETF that focuses on renewable energy, technology, or international markets.

Reflect on whether ETFs align with your investment style. Are you looking for flexibility and low costs? If so, ETFs could be a valuable addition to your portfolio.

Real Estate: Investing Beyond the Stock Market

Real estate is another popular investment option that offers the potential for long-term growth. Whether it's buying rental properties, flipping houses, or investing in real estate investment trusts (REITs), real estate allows you to diversify your portfolio and generate income through rent or property appreciation.

While real estate can require a larger upfront investment and ongoing maintenance, it also provides tangible value and potential tax benefits. Reflect on your interest in real estate and whether it aligns with your financial goals and risk tolerance.

Balancing Risk and Reward

Every investment carries some level of risk, and the key to successful investing is finding the right balance between risk and reward. Younger investors with more time to recover from market fluctuations might lean toward riskier assets like stocks, while those closer to retirement might prioritize stability with bonds or cash equivalents.

Take some time to reflect on your personal risk tolerance. How do you feel about market ups and downs? Are you comfortable with short-term losses in exchange for potential long-term gains? Your answers will guide your investment strategy and help you choose the right mix of assets.

The Importance of Time

One of the most powerful factors in investing is time. The longer you leave your money invested, the more it benefits from compounding returns, where your earnings generate additional earnings. This is why starting early, even with small amounts, can make a significant difference in the long run.

Reflect on your own timeline and goals. What are you saving for, and how long do you have to achieve it? Understanding your time horizon will help you choose the right investment vehicles and stay focused on the bigger picture.

Reflecting on Your Next Steps

Investing can feel intimidating at first, but it's also one of the most empowering steps you can take toward financial independence. Take some time to reflect on what you've learned and how you can apply it to your own financial journey. What investment vehicles resonate with you? How can you start incorporating them into your savings plan?

Balancing Risk and Reward

When it comes to saving and investing, balancing risk and reward is at the heart of creating a plan that works for you. This balance is about aligning your financial decisions with your goals, your timeline, and your comfort level. It's not about taking unnecessary risks or playing it so safe that you miss opportunities. Instead, it's about finding a strategy that feels right for where you are today and where you want to go.

Understanding Risk and Reward

At its core, risk refers to the uncertainty of an investment's return. Some investments, like stocks, have the potential for higher returns but also come with greater risk. Others, like bonds or high-yield savings accounts, offer more stability but generally lower returns. Reward is the potential gain from your investment—the reason you're willing to accept some level of risk in the first place.

The key is recognizing that every financial decision involves some level of risk, even choosing not to invest. By avoiding investments altogether, you risk missing out on growth opportunities and falling short of your long-term goals.

Reflect on your current approach to risk. Are you someone who prefers security and stability, or are you open to taking on more risk for the chance of higher rewards? Understanding where you fall on this spectrum will help you build a strategy that feels right for you.

Knowing Your Risk Tolerance

Risk tolerance is your ability and willingness to endure fluctuations in the value of your investments. It's influenced by factors like your financial situation, your goals, and your personality. Some people are comfortable with the ups and downs of the stock market, while others lose sleep over even minor losses.

Take a moment to reflect on how you've reacted to financial risks in the past. Have you ever made an investment, like buying a house or starting a business? How did it feel? Did you thrive on the excitement, or did the uncertainty cause stress? Your past experiences can offer valuable insight into your risk tolerance.

If you're not sure where you stand, consider asking yourself these questions: How much of a loss could I handle without feeling anxious? How much time do I have to recover from potential losses? How important is growth versus stability in my overall financial plan? Your answers will guide you toward a strategy that aligns with your comfort level.

Matching Risk to Your Goals

Different financial goals require different levels of risk. Short-term goals, like saving for a vacation or an emergency fund, are best suited to low-risk options like high-yield savings accounts or certificates of deposit (CDs). These tools protect your principal while offering modest growth.

Long-term goals, like retirement or building wealth, often require higher-risk investments like stocks or mutual funds. Over time, these investments have the potential to generate higher returns, helping you stay ahead of inflation and achieve your goals.

Reflect on your own goals and their timelines. Are you saving for something in the next few years, or are you planning decades into the future? Matching the risk level of your investments to your goals ensures that your strategy is both practical and effective.

Diversifying to Manage Risk

One of the best ways to balance risk and reward is through diversification. This means spreading your money across different types of investments, industries, and geographic regions. By doing so, you reduce the impact of any single investment's poor performance on your overall portfolio.

For example, instead of putting all your money into a single stock, you could invest in a mix of stocks, bonds, and exchange-traded funds (ETFs). This approach helps smooth out the ups and downs of individual investments, making your portfolio more resilient.

Think of diversification as creating a safety net. Reflect on whether your current savings and investments are concentrated in one area or spread out. If they're concentrated, consider how diversifying could provide more balance and stability.

Adjusting Over Time

Your risk tolerance and financial goals can change as your life evolves. When you're young and just starting out, you might be more willing to take risks because you have time to recover from losses. As you approach retirement or other major milestones, your focus may shift to preserving wealth and minimizing risk.

This process, known as rebalancing, involves adjusting your portfolio periodically to maintain the right balance of risk and reward. For example, you might reduce your exposure to stocks and increase your allocation to bonds as you get closer to retirement.

Reflect on where you are in your financial journey. Are your investments aligned with your current stage of life? If not, what changes could you make to ensure your strategy supports your goals and comfort level?

Staying Emotionally Balanced

Investing can be an emotional experience, especially when markets are volatile. It's natural to feel excited when your investments are performing well and anxious when they're not. But making decisions based on emotions rather than strategy can lead to mistakes, like selling during a downturn or chasing high-risk investments during a boom.

Staying balanced means focusing on your long-term goals rather than short-term market movements. Reflect on how you've handled financial challenges in the past. Did you react impulsively, or were you able to stay calm and stick to your plan? Use these experiences to build a strategy that helps you manage emotions and make decisions based on logic and goals.

Taking Small Steps

If you're new to investing or unsure about taking on risk, start small. You don't have to go all-in on stocks or high-risk assets right away. Begin with conservative options like bonds or balanced mutual funds, and gradually increase your exposure to higher-risk investments as you become more comfortable.

Starting small allows you to learn and gain confidence without putting too much at stake. Reflect on how you feel about taking your first steps into investing. What small actions could you take today to begin building a portfolio that balances risk and reward?

Chapter 7

Paying Down Debt While Saving

The Impact of Debt on Savings

Debt is a reality for many people, and while it can be a useful tool when managed wisely, high-interest debt can create significant challenges. It can feel like a heavy weight, slowing your financial progress and making it harder to achieve your goals. When you're focused on paying off debt, building savings often takes a backseat, and the longer debt lingers, the more it can erode your ability to grow wealth. Understanding how high-interest debt affects your financial health is the first step toward regaining control and creating a balanced plan for both repayment and saving.

The Cycle of High-Interest Debt

High-interest debt, like credit card balances or payday loans, can create a cycle that's hard to break. When interest accumulates faster than you can pay it off, your debt grows even if you're making payments. This cycle eats into your income, leaving less room for savings or other financial goals.

For example, imagine carrying a $5,000 credit card balance with an interest rate of 20%. If you make only the minimum payment each month, it could take years to pay off the debt—and you might end up paying thousands of dollars in interest alone. That's money that could have been used to build an emergency fund, invest, or achieve other milestones.

Reflect on your own financial situation. Have you ever felt like your debt payments were holding you back from saving? Recognizing this dynamic is an important step toward finding solutions that work for you.

How Debt Reduces Your Financial Flexibility

One of the biggest impacts of debt is the way it limits your financial flexibility. When a large portion of your income goes toward debt payments, it becomes harder to handle unexpected expenses or take advantage of opportunities. Without savings to fall back on, you might find yourself relying on more debt, which only deepens the cycle.

Debt can also make it harder to pursue long-term goals. If you're focused on paying off loans or credit cards, you might feel like you can't afford to save for a down payment on a house, contribute to retirement accounts, or invest in education or career growth. This delay in reaching your goals can be discouraging, but it's important to remember that every small step toward paying down debt brings you closer to financial freedom.

The Emotional Toll of Debt

Debt isn't just a financial burden—it's an emotional one, too. The stress of keeping up with payments, worrying about interest, and feeling like you're falling behind can take a toll on your mental and emotional well-being. It's easy to feel overwhelmed, especially if you're unsure how to balance debt repayment with saving for the future.

These feelings of stress and overwhelm are valid, but they don't have to define your financial journey. Reflect on how debt has impacted you emotionally. Has it made you feel stuck or limited? Acknowledging these emotions can help you approach your financial plan with compassion and clarity.

The Opportunity Cost of High-Interest Debt

Every dollar spent on interest is a dollar that isn't going toward building your savings or achieving your goals. This is the opportunity cost of debt—the hidden cost of what you're missing out on. For example, instead of earning interest in a high-yield savings account or growing your money through investments, you're paying interest to a lender.

This doesn't mean you should feel guilty about your debt. Many people face unexpected challenges, like medical bills or job loss, that lead to borrowing. The important thing is to recognize the impact and create a plan to minimize the opportunity cost going forward.

Reflect on the goals you want to achieve. How might paying off high-interest debt free up resources to pursue those dreams? Visualizing what's possible can motivate you to tackle your debt with purpose.

Breaking Free from the Debt Trap

It's easy to feel like debt is a trap you can't escape, but it's important to remember that every small step counts. Start by creating a clear picture of your financial situation. Write down all your debts, including balances, interest rates, and minimum payments. This might feel intimidating, but it's a crucial step toward regaining control.

Once you have a clear understanding of your debt, prioritize tackling high-interest accounts first. These debts cost you the most over time, so paying them down aggressively can save you money and free up income for savings. Consider whether consolidating your debt or negotiating lower interest rates with creditors might help you make faster progress.

Reflect on how you've handled debt in the past. What strategies have worked for you, and where have you struggled? Use these insights to create a plan that feels manageable and aligned with your financial goals.

Balancing Debt Repayment with Saving

One of the biggest challenges of managing debt is deciding how to balance repayment with saving. It's tempting to focus entirely on paying off debt, but having some savings—especially an emergency fund—can prevent you from relying on more debt when unexpected expenses arise.

Start by setting a small, achievable savings goal, like $500 or $1,000. This fund acts as a buffer while you work on reducing your debt. Once you've built this safety net, shift more focus to paying off high-interest debt. Reflect on how it feels to have even a small amount of savings set aside. Does it give you peace of mind and motivation to keep going?

The Power of Mindset

Debt can feel overwhelming, but shifting your mindset can make a big difference. Instead of seeing debt as a burden, try viewing it as a challenge you're capable of overcoming. Every payment you make, no matter how small, is a step toward financial freedom. Celebrate your progress and remind yourself that you're taking control of your future.

Reflect on your relationship with debt. How do you feel about it, and how has it shaped your financial habits? By approaching debt with a growth mindset, you can turn it into an opportunity to learn, grow, and build a stronger foundation for the future.

Debt Repayment Strategies

When you're ready to tackle your debt, having a clear strategy makes all the difference. Two of the most popular methods for paying off debt faster are the snowball method and the avalanche method. Both have their strengths, and the right choice depends on your personal preferences, goals, and financial situation. Let's explore these approaches, how they work, and how you can decide which one is best for you.

The Snowball Method: Building Momentum

The snowball method focuses on building confidence and motivation by starting with your smallest debt. With this strategy, you list your debts in order from the smallest balance to the largest, regardless of interest rate. You pay the minimum on all your debts except the smallest, where you apply any extra money you can. Once the smallest debt is paid off, you roll that payment amount into the next smallest debt, and so on.

The idea is simple: by eliminating smaller debts first, you experience quick wins that keep you motivated to continue. The sense of accomplishment from paying off a debt completely can be incredibly empowering, especially if you've struggled with staying consistent in the past.

Imagine this process as a snowball rolling down a hill. It starts small but grows larger and gains momentum as it picks up speed. Each small victory builds your confidence and helps you believe that becoming debt-free is possible.

Reflect on your own financial journey. Have you found it easier to stay motivated when you see immediate results? If so, the snowball method might be the right fit for you.

The Avalanche Method: Saving on Interest

The avalanche method takes a more mathematical approach, prioritizing debts with the highest interest rates first. With this strategy, you list your debts in order of interest rate, starting with the highest. You pay the minimum on all your debts except the one with the highest interest, where you direct any extra money. Once that debt is paid off, you move on to the next highest interest rate.

This approach minimizes the total amount of interest you pay over time, which can save you money in the long run. It's especially effective if you're dealing with high-interest debts like credit cards or payday loans.

Think of the avalanche method as an efficient way to tackle your debt strategically. By focusing on the highest interest rates first, you reduce the overall cost of your debt and free up more money to apply to other balances.

Reflect on your financial goals. Are you focused on saving as much money as possible while paying off debt? If so, the avalanche method could align better with your priorities.

Comparing the Two Methods

The snowball and avalanche methods share the same goal: eliminating debt as quickly and effectively as possible. The difference lies in their approach—one prioritizes psychological wins, while the other emphasizes financial savings. The key is to choose the method that feels most manageable and motivating for you.

The snowball method is particularly helpful if you're struggling to stay consistent with your debt repayment plan. Those quick wins create a positive feedback loop, making it easier to stick with your plan. However, the downside is that you may pay more in interest over time, especially if you have large high-interest debts that take longer to address.

The avalanche method is ideal if you're comfortable staying focused on long-term savings. It's the more cost-effective approach, as you'll pay less interest overall. But it requires discipline and patience, as the highest-interest debt might also be the largest, meaning it could take longer to see significant progress.

Reflect on your personality and financial habits. Do you thrive on immediate results, or are you willing to wait for bigger payoffs? Your answers will help guide your decision.

Combining the Two Strategies

If neither method feels like a perfect fit, consider combining them. For example, you could start with the snowball method to build momentum and then switch to the avalanche method once you've gained confidence and established a repayment routine. This hybrid approach allows you to balance motivation with financial efficiency.

Reflect on how you might customize your debt repayment plan. Could a combination of snowball and avalanche strategies help you stay motivated while also saving on interest? Flexibility is key to finding a plan that works for you.

Staying Consistent with Your Plan

No matter which method you choose, consistency is the most important factor in paying off debt faster. Set a budget that prioritizes debt repayment and look for ways to free up extra money to accelerate your progress. Celebrate your milestones along the way, whether it's paying off your smallest debt or eliminating a high-interest balance.

Reflect on what motivates you to stay consistent. Is it the vision of a debt-free future? The relief of having more financial freedom? Keep these motivations front and center as you work toward your goals.

Saving While Managing Debt

On one hand, paying off debt can reduce financial stress and free up money in your budget. On the other, having savings provides security and peace of mind, protecting you from falling into more debt when unexpected expenses arise. It's not about choosing one over the other—it's about finding the balance that works for you, so you can make progress in both areas without feeling overwhelmed.

Why Balancing Savings and Debt Matters

When you're focused solely on paying off debt, it's easy to neglect savings. But this approach can leave you vulnerable. Without an emergency fund, even a small, unexpected expense could push you back into debt. At the same time, directing all your money toward savings while neglecting high-interest debt can cost you more in the long run, as interest accumulates and makes your debt harder to pay off.

The balance lies in addressing both needs simultaneously. By allocating resources to both savings and debt repayment, you create a financial foundation that supports your long-term goals. It's not about perfection—it's about consistent, intentional progress.

Starting with an Emergency Fund

Building a small emergency fund is the first step to balancing savings and debt. Even having $500 or $1,000 set aside can prevent you from relying on credit cards or loans when unexpected expenses come up. This small cushion provides peace of mind and allows you to focus more confidently on tackling your debt.

Reflect on your current financial situation. How would having a small emergency fund change the way you feel about your money? Would it give you more confidence to face challenges or unexpected events?

To build your emergency fund while managing debt, start small. Look for ways to free up even $10 or $20 a week to put into savings. Whether it's cutting back on dining out, pausing a subscription, or selling items you no longer need, these small steps add up over time.

Creating a Budget That Supports Both Goals

A clear, realistic budget is essential for balancing savings and debt repayment. Start by calculating your income and expenses, and identify how much you can allocate to each goal. Your budget should reflect your priorities, with room for both debt payments and savings contributions.

One effective approach is the "50/30/20 rule," where 50% of your income goes to needs, 30% to wants, and 20% to savings and debt repayment. Depending on your financial situation, you might adjust this ratio to direct more toward debt or savings as needed.

Reflect on your own budget. Are you allocating resources in a way that aligns with your goals? If not, what adjustments could you make to create a more balanced plan?

Paying Off High-Interest Debt First

High-interest debt, like credit cards or payday loans, can significantly hinder your ability to save. The interest adds up quickly, leaving less room in your budget for other priorities. Prioritizing high-interest debt while maintaining small savings contributions can help you make faster progress.

For example, you might use the avalanche method to focus on debts with the highest interest rates while still contributing to your emergency fund. This approach minimizes the total cost of your debt while ensuring you have some savings in place for emergencies.

Reflect on your own debts. Are there high-interest accounts you could prioritize to free up more money for savings? Taking a strategic approach to repayment can accelerate your progress.

Automating Savings and Debt Payments

Automation is a powerful tool for managing both savings and debt. By setting up automatic transfers to your savings account and scheduling debt payments, you ensure that both goals are addressed consistently. Automation removes the temptation to skip payments or divert money elsewhere, keeping you on track.

Reflect on how automation could simplify your financial routine. Would it reduce stress and make it easier to stay consistent? Even small, automated contributions to savings or debt can have a significant impact over time.

Staying Flexible with Your Plan

Life is unpredictable, and there may be times when you need to adjust your plan. For example, if an emergency arises, you might need to pause extra debt payments to rebuild your savings. Or, if you receive a windfall, you could use part of it to make a larger debt payment while setting aside the rest for savings.

Flexibility is key to balancing savings and debt. Reflect on how you've handled financial challenges in the past. Did you feel prepared, or did unexpected events throw you off course? Use these reflections to create a plan that allows for adjustments without losing sight of your goals.

Building Momentum with Small Wins

Balancing savings and debt can feel overwhelming, but focusing on small wins can keep you motivated. Celebrate every milestone, whether it's paying off a credit card, reaching your first $500 in savings, or sticking to your budget for a full month. These achievements reinforce the progress you're making and remind you that every step counts.

Reflect on your recent financial accomplishments. What are you proud of, and how can you build on that momentum? Acknowledging your efforts helps you stay motivated and focused.

Reflecting on Your Priorities

As you work to balance savings and debt, take time to reflect on your financial priorities. What matters most to you—security, freedom, stability? How do your goals align with these values? By keeping your priorities in mind, you can create a plan that feels meaningful and sustainable.

Chapter 8

Planning for Retirement

Why Retirement Savings Are Crucial

Retirement might seem like a distant chapter in your life, but the decisions you make today will shape how comfortable and secure that chapter becomes. Saving for retirement is more than just setting money aside—it's about creating the freedom to live your life on your terms, without financial stress or uncertainty. While it's easy to put off retirement planning in favor of more immediate priorities, starting now can make a significant difference in your future.

Securing Your Future Comfort and Freedom

Think about what retirement means to you. Is it traveling the world, spending quality time with family, pursuing hobbies, or simply enjoying a slower pace of life? Whatever your vision, having sufficient savings ensures you can pursue it without worrying about how to cover basic expenses. Retirement savings act as a financial cushion, giving you the freedom to make choices that align with your dreams.

Without adequate savings, retirement can feel more like a struggle than a reward. Social Security benefits, while helpful, are rarely enough to cover all expenses. Having your own savings allows you to bridge the gap and maintain the lifestyle you've worked so hard to build.

Reflect on the kind of life you want in retirement. How would having financial security enhance your ability to enjoy it? Visualizing your future can help you stay motivated to save consistently.

The Power of Time and Consistency

One of the most compelling reasons to start saving for retirement now is the power of time. The earlier you begin, the more time your money has to grow through compound interest, where your earnings generate even more earnings. Even small, consistent contributions made early can result in substantial savings over the long term.

For example, let's say you start saving $200 a month at age 25 and continue until age 65. Assuming an average annual return of 7%, you'd have nearly $480,000 by retirement. If you wait until age 35 to start saving the same amount, your total would drop to around $240,000—half as much, even though you saved for only 10 fewer years.

Reflect on your current savings habits. Are you making regular contributions to a retirement account? If not, what steps can you take to start building momentum? Even if your budget is tight, starting with a small amount can make a big difference over time.

Preparing for Longer Life Expectancy

Advances in healthcare mean people are living longer than ever before, and while that's something to celebrate, it also means your retirement savings need to last longer. The average retirement can span 20 to 30 years or more, depending on when you retire and your overall health.

Having a solid retirement plan ensures you won't outlive your savings. It provides peace of mind, knowing you'll be able to cover healthcare costs, daily living expenses, and unexpected needs without compromising your quality of life.

Reflect on how your health and lifestyle might impact your retirement needs. Are there steps you can take now, such as contributing more to your savings or exploring additional income streams, to prepare for a longer retirement?

Reducing Financial Stress for Loved Ones

Saving for retirement isn't just about securing your own future—it's also about protecting your loved ones from financial stress. Without adequate savings, you may need to rely on family members for support, which can strain relationships and add stress to their lives.

Having your own financial independence allows you to maintain your dignity and freedom while giving your loved ones peace of mind. It ensures that you can contribute to family activities, help with grandkids, or simply enjoy time together without money being a concern.

Reflect on how having financial independence in retirement would impact your relationships with loved ones. What steps can you take now to ensure you're prepared for both your needs and theirs?

Navigating Uncertainty

Life is full of uncertainties, and retirement is no exception. From economic fluctuations to healthcare costs, there are many variables that can impact your financial stability in retirement. Having a robust savings plan helps you weather these uncertainties with confidence.

For example, healthcare expenses are a significant concern for retirees. While Medicare provides some coverage, it doesn't cover everything, and out-of-pocket costs can add up quickly. Having a dedicated savings fund for healthcare ensures you can access the care you need without compromising other aspects of your lifestyle.

Reflect on the uncertainties you might face in retirement. Are there specific areas, like healthcare or housing, that you feel unprepared for? Taking proactive steps now can reduce these worries and help you approach retirement with confidence.

Overcoming Barriers to Saving

It's common to feel like there are too many competing priorities to focus on retirement savings. Between paying bills, managing debt, and handling day-to-day expenses, it can feel impossible to set aside extra money. But even small changes can create room in your budget for savings.

Start by examining your spending habits. Are there areas where you could cut back, even slightly, to free up money for your future? Reflect on the barriers you've faced in prioritizing retirement savings. What small adjustments could you make today to start building momentum?

Reflecting on Your Commitment to Your Future

Saving for retirement is a long-term commitment, but it's one of the most empowering decisions you can make. It's about prioritizing your future self and creating a life of comfort, security, and freedom. Every dollar you save today brings you closer to that vision.

Take a moment to reflect on your retirement goals. What does a comfortable and fulfilling retirement look like to you? How can saving now help you achieve it? By staying connected to your "why," you'll find the motivation to make consistent contributions and build a brighter future.

Exploring Retirement Accounts

Retirement savings are one of the most impactful ways to secure your future, and choosing the right retirement accounts is key to maximizing your efforts. Options like 401(k)s, IRAs, and Roth IRAs are designed to help you grow your money efficiently, often with significant tax benefits. By understanding how these accounts work and how to use them effectively, you can make informed decisions that align with your financial goals.

What Is a 401(k) Plan?

A 401(k) is an employer-sponsored retirement account that allows you to contribute a portion of your salary to savings before taxes are deducted. This tax advantage means that contributions reduce your taxable income, giving you immediate savings while growing your retirement fund. Over time, the money you contribute grows tax-deferred, meaning you don't pay taxes on it until you withdraw funds in retirement.

One of the most compelling features of a 401(k) is the potential for employer matching. Many companies match a percentage of your contributions, effectively giving you free money toward your retirement. For example, if your employer matches 50% of your contributions up to 6% of your salary and you earn $50,000 annually, contributing $3,000 could result in an additional $1,500 from your employer.

Reflect on whether you're currently taking advantage of a 401(k) plan. If your employer offers matching, are you contributing enough to get the full benefit? Maximizing this match is one of the best ways to accelerate your retirement savings.

Traditional IRA: A Tax-Deferred Option

An Individual Retirement Account (IRA) is another popular option for retirement savings, particularly if your employer doesn't offer a 401(k). A traditional IRA allows you to contribute pre-tax income, and like a 401(k), the funds grow tax-deferred. This means you don't pay taxes on the money until you withdraw it in retirement.

The contribution limit for traditional IRAs is generally lower than for 401(k)s, but they offer more flexibility. You can open an IRA on your own, giving you control over where and how you invest your money. Traditional IRAs are especially useful for people who anticipate being in a lower tax bracket during retirement, as they'll pay less tax on withdrawals.

Reflect on whether a traditional IRA might be a good fit for your financial situation. Do you prefer the flexibility of managing your own investments, or would you benefit more from an employer-sponsored plan? Understanding your preferences and tax situation will help you decide.

Roth IRA: Tax-Free Growth

A Roth IRA is similar to a traditional IRA, but with a key difference—contributions are made with after-tax income. While this means you don't get an immediate tax break, the money grows tax-free, and withdrawals in retirement are also tax-free. This can be a significant advantage if you expect to be in a higher tax bracket in the future or want to minimize taxes on your retirement income.

Roth IRAs also offer more flexibility than traditional IRAs when it comes to withdrawals. You can withdraw your contributions (but not earnings) at any time without penalty, making it a useful option if you anticipate needing access to some of your savings before retirement.

Reflect on whether a Roth IRA aligns with your goals. Are you willing to forgo the upfront tax benefit for the long-term advantage of tax-free withdrawals? This choice often depends on your current income and your expectations for the future.

Choosing Between a Traditional IRA and Roth IRA

Deciding between a traditional IRA and a Roth IRA often comes down to your current income, tax situation, and retirement goals. If you're in a higher tax bracket now and expect to be in a lower one during retirement, a traditional IRA may offer more immediate tax savings. On the other hand, if you're in a lower tax bracket now and anticipate higher income or tax rates in retirement, a Roth IRA can be a smarter choice.

Reflect on your current and future tax situation. Do you expect your income to increase over time? How might tax rates change? These questions can help guide your decision between these two powerful savings options.

Combining Accounts for Maximum Benefit

You're not limited to just one type of retirement account. Many people find that combining accounts—such as contributing to both a 401(k) and an IRA—provides the best balance of tax advantages and savings potential. For example, you could maximize your employer's 401(k) match while also contributing to a Roth IRA for tax-free growth.

Reflect on whether you're currently using multiple accounts to optimize your retirement savings. If not, what steps could you take to explore additional options? A diversified approach often offers the best chance of achieving your goals.

Exploring Other Retirement Accounts

While 401(k)s and IRAs are the most common retirement accounts, there are other options worth considering, especially if you're self-employed or looking for additional ways to save.

If you're self-employed or own a small business, options like a SEP IRA or a Solo 401(k) can provide significant tax advantages and higher contribution limits. These accounts allow you to save more aggressively while still enjoying the tax benefits of traditional retirement accounts.

Reflect on your current employment situation. Could these specialized accounts help you save more effectively? Exploring less common options can open new doors for your retirement planning.

Making Regular Contributions

The key to building a strong retirement fund is consistency. Even small, regular contributions can grow significantly over time thanks to compound interest. Automating your contributions ensures that saving becomes a habit, reducing the temptation to skip or delay payments.

Reflect on your current contribution habits. Are you saving consistently, or could you benefit from automating your payments? Building a routine around your retirement savings helps ensure steady progress.

Staying Informed and Flexible

Retirement planning isn't a one-time decision—it's an ongoing process. Tax laws, contribution limits, and investment options can change over time, so staying informed is crucial. Regularly reviewing your accounts and adjusting your strategy ensures that your plan remains aligned with your goals.

Reflect on how often you review your retirement accounts. Are there opportunities to increase your contributions, adjust your investments, or explore new options? Staying proactive helps you make the most of your savings.

Reflecting on Your Goals

Retirement accounts are more than just financial tools—they're vehicles for achieving your dreams. Take a moment to reflect on what retirement means to you and how these accounts can help you get there. Are you focused on building a comfortable lifestyle, leaving a legacy for loved ones, or pursuing passions that require financial freedom? Understanding your "why" keeps you motivated and on track.

Starting Early, Saving More

When it comes to saving for the future, time is one of your greatest allies. The earlier you start, the more your money can grow, thanks to the power of compound interest. Compound interest is often called the "eighth wonder of the world" for a reason—it allows your savings to grow exponentially over time, turning even small contributions into significant wealth. Understanding how it works and why starting early matters can inspire you to take action today, no matter where you are on your financial journey.

What Is Compound Interest?

At its core, compound interest is the process of earning interest not only on your original investment but also on the interest that accumulates over time. This creates a snowball effect, where your savings grow faster the longer they're invested. Unlike simple interest, which only earns on the initial principal, compound interest accelerates growth by reinvesting earnings into your balance.

Imagine depositing $1,000 in a savings account that earns 5% annual interest. In the first year, you earn $50 in interest, bringing your total to $1,050. In the second year, that 5% applies to the new total, so you earn $52.50, and your balance grows to $1,102.50. Over time, the growth becomes increasingly significant, with your money working harder for you each year.

Reflect on the idea of your money working for you. How does it feel to know that even small amounts can grow substantially with time and consistency?

The Impact of Starting Early

One of the most powerful aspects of compound interest is how it rewards those who start saving early. The longer your money has to grow, the more pronounced the compounding effect becomes. Even if you can only save a small amount at first, starting early gives you a head start that's difficult to replicate later.

Consider two people, Alex and Jordan. Alex starts saving $100 a month at age 25 and stops at age 35, while Jordan starts saving $100 a month at age 35 and continues until age 65. Assuming a 7% annual return, Alex's savings grow to over $168,000 by age 65, despite saving for only 10 years. Jordan, on the other hand, saves for 30 years but ends up with just over $120,000. The difference lies in the extra time Alex's money had to grow.

Reflect on your own financial timeline. Are you taking full advantage of the time you have to let your money grow? If not, what small steps could you take today to get started?

Small Contributions Add Up

One common misconception is that you need a large amount of money to benefit from compound interest. In reality, even modest contributions can add up significantly over time. The key is consistency. By saving regularly, whether it's $10, $50, or $100 a month, you build a habit that leads to long-term success.

Think about a coffee habit, where you might spend $4 a day. Redirecting that money into savings could add up to over $1,200 a year. Invested at a 7% return, that $1,200 could grow to nearly $17,000 in 10 years and over $120,000 in 30 years. Reflect on how small changes in your spending habits could open up opportunities to save more and maximize your financial growth.

Compound Interest and Retirement Savings

Retirement accounts like 401(k)s, IRAs, and Roth IRAs are designed to take full advantage of compound interest. Contributions are often made consistently, and the tax advantages allow your money to grow faster compared to taxable accounts. Over decades, this growth can create a substantial nest egg that supports your future.

Think about your current contributions to retirement accounts. Are you taking full advantage of employer matches, tax benefits, and compounding? If not, what adjustments could you make to boost your savings and reap the rewards of long-term growth?

Overcoming the Challenges of Starting Early

Life can make it difficult to prioritize savings, especially when you're managing other financial goals like paying off debt or covering everyday expenses. But starting small and staying consistent can help you overcome these challenges. Remember, the goal isn't to save a fortune overnight—it's to establish a habit that builds over time.

Reflect on the barriers you've faced in prioritizing savings. Have you felt overwhelmed by competing demands, or uncertain about how to begin? What steps can you take to simplify the process and make saving feel more achievable?

The Cost of Waiting

While starting early offers significant benefits, waiting to save can have equally significant costs. Every year you delay means less time for compounding to work its magic. This can result in needing to save much larger amounts later to reach the same goal.

For example, saving $200 a month starting at age 25 with an 8% return would grow to over $700,000 by age 65. Waiting until age 35 to start saving the same amount reduces the total to around $350,000. Reflect on how waiting might impact your own goals. What would starting now mean for your future?

Staying Motivated Over Time

The long-term nature of compound interest requires patience and persistence. It's easy to lose motivation when progress feels slow at first, but staying committed to your savings plan ensures that you'll reap the rewards down the line. Celebrate small milestones, like reaching your first $1,000 in savings, and remind yourself of the bigger picture.

Reflect on what keeps you motivated to save. Is it the vision of a comfortable retirement, the freedom to travel, or the ability to support loved ones? Staying connected to your goals makes the journey more rewarding.

Reflecting on Your Next Steps

Understanding the power of compound interest is an invitation to take action. Whether you're just starting out or looking to optimize your current savings strategy, every step you take today brings you closer to financial freedom. Reflect on what you've learned and how you can apply it to your own life. Are there opportunities to start saving more, automate contributions, or explore higher-yield investments?

Chapter 9

Saving for Your Family's Future

Teaching Financial Literacy to Children

Financial literacy is one of the most important skills a child can learn. Teaching children about saving, spending, and earning money equips them with the tools to make informed decisions and avoid common financial pitfalls later in life. Instilling these habits early helps them develop confidence, responsibility, and a sense of empowerment when managing money. In this chapter, we'll explore how you can teach your child the value of saving, provide actionable tips for making financial lessons engaging, and create a foundation for lifelong financial success.

Starting Early with Simple Concepts

The sooner children are introduced to money management, the more natural it becomes for them to adopt good habits. Even toddlers can begin to grasp the concept of saving when they see money being put into a piggy bank. The key is to start small and use tangible, everyday examples that resonate with their level of understanding.

For young children, a piggy bank or savings jar can be a great visual tool. Each time they add money, talk about how saving helps them work toward something they really want. For instance, if they're saving for a new toy, help them see the connection between each coin and getting closer to their goal. This makes the act of saving more meaningful and exciting.

Reflect on the lessons you wish you'd learned about money when you were younger. How might those lessons have changed your financial habits today? Passing those insights to your children ensures they're better prepared for their own financial journeys.

Encouraging Earning Opportunities

Children appreciate money more when they've earned it themselves. Giving them opportunities to earn money not only builds their confidence but also teaches them the value of hard work. You can start by assigning age-appropriate chores, offering small allowances in return for completed tasks, or helping them set up a lemonade stand or other entrepreneurial venture.

Once your child earns money, guide them in deciding what to do with it. Encourage them to divide their earnings into three categories: saving, spending, and giving. For example, they could save a portion for long-term goals, spend a portion on something fun, and donate a portion to a cause they care about. This simple system introduces the idea of financial balance and responsibility.

Reflect on how earning their own money could shape your child's understanding of value and effort. What creative ways could you introduce opportunities for them to earn and manage their funds?

Setting Savings Goals Together

Children are more likely to embrace saving when it's tied to a specific goal. Sit down with your child and talk about something they'd like to save for. It could be a toy, a special outing, or even a larger goal like a bike or video game console. Write the goal down and create a savings tracker, such as a chart or a jar with markings, so they can see their progress.

As they work toward their goal, celebrate milestones along the way. For instance, if they've saved half the amount needed, acknowledge their effort and talk about how much closer they are to achieving their goal. These celebrations reinforce the idea that saving is rewarding and worthwhile.

Reflect on the goals you've worked toward in your own life. How did reaching those goals make you feel? Sharing these experiences with your child helps them see the value of perseverance and planning.

Teaching Through Real-Life Examples

One of the best ways to teach financial literacy is by involving your child in real-life situations. For instance, when you're at the grocery store, explain how you compare prices to find the best value. When planning a family outing, talk about the budget you've set and how you're saving for it.

These everyday moments help your child see how financial concepts apply in the real world. They also show that managing money is a normal part of life, not something to be feared or avoided.

Reflect on the financial habits you're modelling for your child. Are there opportunities to involve them more in your decision-making process? Transparency and openness build trust and understanding.

Using Technology to Teach Saving

Today's digital tools make it easier than ever to teach children about money. Many apps are specifically designed to help kids learn financial literacy through interactive games and activities. These apps often include features like virtual piggy banks, savings trackers, and goal-setting tools, making learning fun and engaging.

Consider introducing your child to an age-appropriate app that reinforces the concepts you're teaching at home. These tools can complement your efforts and give them hands-on experience managing virtual money.

Reflect on how technology has changed the way financial literacy is taught. Are there tools or resources that could enhance your child's understanding and make learning more interactive?

Explaining Banking Basics

As your child gets older, introducing them to basic banking concepts helps prepare them for financial independence. Consider opening a savings account in their name and teaching them how to use it. Show them how to make deposits, review account statements, and track the interest their money earns.

You can also explain the concept of interest in simple terms. For example, describe how the bank pays them for keeping their money in the account, and illustrate how that money grows over time. This introduces them to the idea of long-term savings and the benefits of letting money work for them.

Reflect on your own experience with banking. How did you learn about savings accounts, and what do you wish you'd known earlier? Sharing these insights helps your child navigate their first banking experiences with confidence.

Encouraging Open Discussions About Money

Encourage your child to ask questions about money and make it a topic that's safe to discuss. Whether they're curious about how you set a budget, pay bills, or decide on big purchases, use their questions as teaching moments. By normalizing conversations about money, you help them develop a healthy relationship with it.

For example, if your child asks why you're using coupons at the store, explain how small savings add up and allow you to put more money toward other priorities. These small, everyday lessons build a strong foundation of financial literacy.

Reflect on how open conversations about money might have shaped your own understanding of finances. Are there ways to create a supportive environment where your child feels comfortable exploring these concepts?

Teaching the Value of Delayed Gratification

One of the most valuable lessons children can learn about money is the concept of delayed gratification. Saving for something over time, rather than buying it immediately, teaches them patience and discipline. It also helps them understand that financial success often requires planning and effort.

Use small examples to illustrate this concept. For instance, if your child wants a toy, talk about how saving a little each week will allow them to buy it without borrowing or overspending. As they see their savings grow and eventually achieve their goal, they'll understand the rewards of waiting.

Reflect on the role delayed gratification has played in your own life. How might teaching this concept to your child shape their approach to money and decision-making?

Reflecting on Your Legacy

As you teach your child about saving, you're not just helping them manage money—you're creating a legacy of financial literacy that can be passed down through generations. Reflect on the values and lessons you want to instill and how they align with your family's goals and priorities.

Every small step you take to teach your child about money contributes to their lifelong success. Celebrate the progress you're making and trust that your efforts are laying the groundwork for a brighter, more secure future for them. Keep going—you're giving your child a gift that will last a lifetime.

Planning for Education Expenses

Saving for education expenses is one of the most impactful ways to invest in your child's future. The rising cost of college has made planning ahead more important than ever. A well-thought-out strategy can help you reduce the financial burden, avoid taking on unnecessary debt, and give your child the gift of educational opportunities without the stress of overwhelming costs. Among the tools available to support these goals, 529 plans stand out as a versatile and tax-advantaged way to save.

Understanding the Importance of Early Planning

The cost of higher education has grown steadily over the years, and projections indicate it will continue to rise. Waiting until your child is close to college age to start saving can leave you scrambling to cover expenses, potentially forcing you to rely on loans that can take years to repay. Starting early, even with small amounts, gives you the advantage of time and compound interest, which can significantly grow your savings over the years.

Think about your child's dreams and ambitions. Whether they aspire to become a doctor, an artist, or an entrepreneur, education is often a critical stepping stone. Reflect on how your efforts today can empower them to pursue those dreams without financial limitations.

What Is a 529 Plan?

A 529 plan is a state-sponsored savings account designed specifically to help families save for education expenses. Named after Section 529 of the Internal Revenue Code, these accounts offer tax advantages that make saving more efficient. Contributions to a 529 plan grow tax-free, and withdrawals are also tax-free when used for qualified education expenses like tuition, books, and room and board.

529 plans come in two main types: prepaid tuition plans and college savings plans. Prepaid tuition plans allow you to lock in today's tuition rates for future attendance at specific schools, while college savings plans operate more like investment accounts, offering the potential for growth based on market performance. Reflect on which type of plan aligns best with your family's goals and comfort level.

Tax Advantages of 529 Plans

One of the biggest benefits of a 529 plan is the tax savings it offers. Contributions to the plan grow tax-free, and when the funds are used for qualified expenses, withdrawals are not subject to federal income tax. Some states also offer additional tax deductions or credits for contributions, making it even more advantageous to save.

Consider how much more challenging saving might feel without these tax benefits. By taking advantage of a 529 plan, you're maximizing every dollar you contribute, allowing your money to work harder for your child's future.

Flexibility of 529 Plans

529 plans are often thought of as tools for saving for college, but they're much more flexible than that. Recent changes in federal law allow 529 funds to be used for a wide range of educational expenses, including K-12 tuition, apprenticeship programs, and even student loan repayment up to certain limits.

This flexibility means that your investment isn't limited to traditional college expenses. If your child decides to pursue a trade school, take certification courses, or explore other non-traditional paths, your savings can still support their education. Reflect on how this flexibility might give you peace of mind as you plan for your child's unique journey.

Starting Small and Staying Consistent

It's easy to feel overwhelmed by the idea of saving thousands of dollars for education expenses, but the key is to start small and stay consistent. Even modest contributions can add up over time, especially when you take advantage of compound growth and tax-free earnings.

Consider setting up automatic contributions to your 529 plan. This ensures you're consistently saving, even if the amounts are small. Reflect on how automation might make the process feel more manageable and help you stay on track toward your goals.

Involving Friends and Family

529 plans offer a unique opportunity for friends and family to contribute to your child's education savings. Many plans allow others to make contributions, making it easy for loved ones to support your efforts. This can be a great alternative to traditional gifts, creating a lasting impact that benefits your child for years to come.

Reflect on how involving your community might amplify your savings efforts. Could birthdays, holidays, or other special occasions become opportunities for loved ones to invest in your child's future?

Understanding Investment Options

College savings plans under the 529 umbrella often include a range of investment options, from conservative portfolios to more aggressive growth strategies. Many plans offer age-based portfolios that automatically adjust the investment mix as your child gets closer to college age, reducing risk as the time for withdrawals approaches.

Reflect on your own risk tolerance and financial goals. Are you comfortable with a more aggressive strategy in the early years, or would a balanced approach better suit your needs? Taking the time to understand your options ensures you're making choices that align with your comfort level and objectives.

Adjusting as Your Child Grows

Education savings isn't a "set it and forget it" process. As your child grows and their educational goals become clearer, you may need to adjust your savings strategy. For instance, if they express interest in attending an out-of-state university, you might need to increase your contributions to account for higher tuition. Alternatively, if they plan to attend a local community college, you could shift your focus to other financial goals.

Reflect on how staying flexible might help you adapt to changing circumstances. Are there ways to periodically review and adjust your plan to ensure it remains aligned with your child's needs and aspirations?

Exploring Alternatives to 529 Plans

While 529 plans are a powerful tool, they're not the only option for saving for education expenses. Other accounts, like Coverdell Education Savings Accounts (ESAs) or custodial accounts under the Uniform Transfers to Minors Act (UTMA), offer additional flexibility but come with different rules and limitations.

Consider how these alternatives might complement your 529 plan or serve as a backup option. Reflect on your family's unique circumstances and how a diversified approach might provide additional security and opportunities.

Teaching Your Child About Saving for Education

Involving your child in the savings process can be a powerful way to teach them about money and responsibility. Talk to them about the importance of education, how much it costs, and the efforts you're making to prepare for their future. Encourage them to contribute to their own savings if possible, whether through part-time work, scholarships, or other means.

Reflect on how these conversations might shape your child's understanding of money and education. Are there ways to make saving feel like a shared family effort, reinforcing the value of teamwork and planning?

Reflecting on Your Progress

Saving for education expenses is a long-term commitment, and it's important to celebrate the progress you've made along the way. Reflect on how far you've come, the strategies that have worked, and the lessons you've learned. Acknowledge the sacrifices and efforts you've made to give your child the best possible start in life.

Building Generational Wealth

Generational wealth is more than just passing down money or assets—it's about creating a lasting legacy that empowers your family to thrive for years to come. It's about providing opportunities, security, and a foundation of financial knowledge that helps future generations achieve stability and success. Whether you're starting from scratch or building on what you've already achieved, creating generational wealth is a goal that requires intentional planning, consistent effort, and a clear vision of the future you want for your family.

Understanding Generational Wealth

Generational wealth refers to the financial resources and assets that are passed down from one generation to the next. This can include tangible items like property, businesses, investments, and savings, as well as intangible assets like financial literacy, work ethic, and a strong understanding of money management. When done thoughtfully, building generational wealth equips your loved ones with the tools and resources they need to achieve their own goals without starting from scratch.

Reflect on the legacy you want to leave for your family. What values and lessons do you hope to pass down? Generational wealth is as much about instilling a mindset of responsibility and growth as it is about accumulating material resources.

The Importance of Long-Term Vision

Building wealth that lasts beyond your lifetime requires a long-term perspective. It's not about quick wins or short-term gains—it's about making decisions today that will benefit your family years, even decades, into the future. This means focusing on sustainable strategies like saving, investing, and preserving assets while avoiding unnecessary risks or debt that could undermine your efforts.

Reflect on your family's current financial situation and where you'd like to see it in the future. What steps can you take today to set the foundation for a stable, prosperous legacy?

Passing Down Financial Knowledge

One of the most powerful ways to build generational wealth is by teaching your family about money. Financial literacy is a key component of long-term success, and instilling these lessons early helps ensure that future generations know how to manage, grow, and protect the wealth you've worked hard to create.

Start by having open, age-appropriate conversations about money with your children and other family members. Share the lessons you've learned, both the successes and the challenges, and encourage them to ask questions and get involved in financial decision-making. Reflect on the financial habits you've modelled for your family. Are there areas where you could provide more guidance or transparency?

Investing for the Future

Investing is a cornerstone of generational wealth because it allows your money to grow over time. Whether through stocks, real estate, mutual funds, or other investment vehicles, a well-diversified portfolio provides a steady stream of growth that can benefit both you and future generations.

Consider involving your family in the investment process. Discuss the importance of patience, diversification, and risk management, and explain how each investment aligns with your family's goals. Reflect on your own investment strategy. Are you maximizing opportunities for growth while maintaining the level of risk you're comfortable with?

Preserving Wealth Through Estate Planning

Estate planning is a critical aspect of building generational wealth. Without a clear plan in place, much of what you've worked for could be lost to taxes, legal fees, or mismanagement. A comprehensive estate plan ensures that your assets are distributed according to your wishes and that your family is protected.

Start by creating a will that outlines how your assets should be handled. Consider setting up trusts to manage wealth and minimize tax liabilities, and designate beneficiaries for retirement accounts and life insurance policies. Reflect on your current estate plan (or lack thereof). Are there steps you can take to ensure your wealth is preserved and passed down efficiently?

The Role of Real Estate in Generational Wealth

Real estate is often a cornerstone of generational wealth because it provides both immediate benefits, like rental income, and long-term appreciation. Owning property gives your family a tangible asset that can be used, sold, or passed down as needed.

Reflect on how real estate might fit into your wealth-building strategy. Are there opportunities to invest in property, either as a primary residence, rental income, or land development? Real estate can be a powerful tool for creating stability and growth.

Building and Preserving a Family Business

If you're an entrepreneur, a family business can be an incredible way to create generational wealth. Not only does it provide financial resources, but it also instills values like hard work, innovation, and collaboration. However, transitioning a business to the next generation requires careful planning to ensure its long-term success.

Reflect on the legacy you want your business to leave. Are there family members interested in taking on leadership roles? What steps can you take to prepare them for success and ensure a smooth transition?

Teaching the Value of Giving Back

Generational wealth isn't just about accumulating resources—it's also about using those resources to make a positive impact. Teaching your family the importance of giving back, whether through charitable donations, volunteering, or supporting community initiatives, creates a legacy of generosity and responsibility.

Reflect on how giving back aligns with your family's values. Are there causes or organizations you want to support, and how can you involve your family in these efforts? A culture of giving creates a sense of purpose and connection that enhances the impact of your wealth.

Reflecting on Your Legacy

Building generational wealth is a journey that requires intention, commitment, and a clear vision of the future. Reflect on what you want your legacy to look like and the steps you can take to make it a reality. Every decision you make today contributes to the foundation of stability, opportunity, and growth for your family.

Chapter 10

Overcoming Financial Challenges

Navigating Unexpected Expenses

Life is unpredictable, and unexpected expenses are a reality that everyone faces. Whether it's a car repair, a medical bill, or an unforeseen household expense, these moments can feel overwhelming, especially if they catch you off guard financially. The good news is that with thoughtful planning, practical strategies, and the right mindset, you can handle emergencies without completely derailing your savings or financial progress.

Building an Emergency Fund as Your First Line of Defense

An emergency fund is your financial safety net. It's a dedicated pool of money that you can tap into when unexpected expenses arise, protecting you from having to rely on credit cards, loans, or dipping into your long-term savings. Even a small emergency fund can make a big difference by providing peace of mind and reducing financial stress.

The key to building an emergency fund is consistency. Start small, setting aside whatever you can afford each month, and prioritize this as an essential part of your budget. Over time, these small contributions add up, and you'll begin to see the security that comes with having a buffer for life's surprises.

Reflect on your current savings habits. Do you have a separate emergency fund? If not, consider starting one today, even if it's just a modest goal of saving $500 to begin with. Every step you take toward building this fund strengthens your financial resilience.

Assessing the Situation Calmly

When an unexpected expense arises, it's easy to feel panicked or overwhelmed. Taking a moment to assess the situation calmly can help you make clear and thoughtful decisions. Start by identifying the exact nature of the expense—how much is needed, when it's due, and whether there are any options for delaying or reducing the cost.

Reflect on how you've handled emergencies in the past. Did you feel prepared, or did the situation catch you off guard? What lessons can you apply to approach future challenges with greater confidence?

Prioritizing Essential Expenses

In the face of an emergency, it's important to distinguish between what's urgent and what can wait. For instance, if a medical bill is due immediately, prioritize it over discretionary spending or less critical expenses. If your car breaks down and you need it to get to work, addressing the repair becomes a priority.

Reflect on how you currently prioritize your expenses. Are there areas where you could cut back temporarily to address an emergency without jeopardizing your financial stability? Being flexible with your budget during challenging times allows you to stay focused on what matters most.

Exploring Payment Options

Many unexpected expenses come with opportunities to negotiate or create payment plans. For example, medical providers often offer instalment plans, and utility companies may have programs for those facing financial hardship. Don't hesitate to reach out and ask about these options—they can provide breathing room and help you avoid using high-interest credit cards or loans.

Reflect on how comfortable you feel advocating for yourself in these situations. Are there resources or support systems you could lean on to navigate these conversations with confidence? Being proactive can make a significant difference in managing unexpected costs.

Leveraging Your Emergency Fund Wisely

When you have an emergency fund in place, the decision to use it should be intentional and thoughtful. While it's there to help you in times of need, avoid using it for non-urgent or discretionary expenses. Treat your emergency fund as a tool for true emergencies, and make a plan to replenish it as soon as possible after using it.

Reflect on how you've used your savings in the past. Were there moments where you wished you'd had a stronger safety net? How can you strengthen your financial habits to ensure your emergency fund remains available for critical needs?

Minimizing the Impact on Long-Term Savings

One of the biggest challenges of handling unexpected expenses is ensuring they don't derail your long-term financial goals. While it's tempting to pause retirement contributions or dip into your investment accounts, this can have long-term consequences that outweigh the short-term benefit. Instead, explore all other options before tapping into these funds.

Reflect on how you balance short-term needs with long-term goals. Are there ways to adjust your approach to emergencies without compromising your future plans? Maintaining a clear focus on your priorities helps you stay on track even during challenging times.

Relying on Community Resources

In moments of financial strain, community resources can provide valuable support. Local organizations, charities, and government programs often help with food, housing, utilities, and other essential expenses. Don't hesitate to explore these resources if you need temporary relief—it's a practical step that allows you to focus on stabilizing your finances.

Reflect on your comfort level with seeking help when needed. Are there ways to familiarize yourself with the resources available in your community? Knowing where to turn in advance can reduce stress during emergencies.

Rebuilding After an Emergency

Once the immediate challenge is addressed, it's important to take steps to rebuild your financial foundation. If you used your emergency fund, create a plan to replenish it gradually. Reflect on what worked well during the situation and what you'd like to improve for the future. These lessons help you strengthen your financial resilience.

Reflect on how you can approach rebuilding with intention. Are there adjustments you can make to your budget or savings habits to prepare for the next unexpected expense? Taking proactive steps reinforces your ability to handle whatever comes your way.

Staying Empowered Through Preparation

The unpredictability of life doesn't have to leave you feeling powerless. By focusing on preparation, building a safety net, and staying adaptable, you're equipping yourself to handle emergencies with confidence. Every step you take to strengthen your financial resilience brings you closer to a future of stability and peace of mind.

Reflect on how you feel about your current level of preparedness. What actions can you take today to build greater confidence in your ability to navigate the unexpected? Empowering yourself through thoughtful planning is a gift to both your present and future self.

Breaking the Paycheck-to-Paycheck Cycle

Living paycheck to paycheck can feel like a never-ending loop, where you're constantly waiting for the next payday to cover expenses. It's a stressful way to live, and it often leaves little room for saving, investing, or planning for the future. The good news is that breaking this cycle is possible with intentional changes, thoughtful strategies, and a commitment to improving your financial habits.

Understanding the Paycheck-to-Paycheck Trap

Living paycheck to paycheck often stems from a combination of insufficient income, high expenses, and a lack of savings. It's a cycle that keeps you focused on short-term needs, making it hard to plan for anything beyond the next bill. Breaking free requires addressing both the practical and emotional aspects of financial stress.

Reflect on your current financial situation. Do you feel like you're just getting by, or are there moments when you can't cover unexpected expenses? Acknowledging where you are is the first step toward making meaningful changes.

Taking Control of Your Cash Flow

The foundation of breaking the cycle is understanding your cash flow—how much money comes in and where it goes. Start by tracking your income and expenses for a month. Write down every bill, purchase, and payment, no matter how small. This gives you a clear picture of your financial habits and identifies areas where you can cut back.

Reflect on how often you review your spending. Are there categories where you tend to overspend or opportunities to save? Awareness of your cash flow is key to creating a budget that works for you.

Creating a Realistic Budget

A budget is your roadmap to financial stability. It helps you allocate your income toward needs, wants, and savings while avoiding overspending. Start with a simple approach, like the 50/30/20 rule: allocate 50% of your income to necessities, 30% to discretionary spending, and 20% to savings or debt repayment.

Reflect on how budgeting makes you feel. Does it seem restrictive, or does it give you a sense of control? Shifting your mindset to view budgeting as a tool for empowerment can make the process more enjoyable and effective.

Building an Emergency Fund

One of the biggest reasons people live paycheck to paycheck is the lack of a safety net. Without an emergency fund, even small, unexpected expenses can derail your finances. Start by saving a modest goal, like $500 or $1,000, and gradually work toward a larger cushion.

Reflect on how having an emergency fund would change your financial outlook. Would it reduce stress and give you more confidence in handling surprises? Making this a priority can help you feel more secure and in control.

Reducing Expenses Thoughtfully

Cutting back on expenses doesn't mean sacrificing your quality of life. It's about identifying areas where you can spend less without feeling deprived. Consider reviewing subscriptions, negotiating bills, or finding more affordable alternatives for daily expenses.

Reflect on the expenses that bring you the most joy and those that feel like wasted money. Are there adjustments you can make to align your spending with what truly matters to you?

Increasing Your Income

Sometimes, breaking the cycle requires more than just cutting expenses—it also involves finding ways to increase your income. This might mean taking on a side hustle, freelancing, or pursuing additional training to qualify for a higher-paying job. Even a small boost in income can make a big difference when combined with better financial habits.

Reflect on your skills and interests. Are there opportunities to monetize a hobby or take on extra work temporarily? Investing in your earning potential can accelerate your progress toward financial freedom.

Prioritizing Debt Repayment

High-interest debt is one of the biggest obstacles to financial stability. It drains your income through interest payments, leaving less room for saving or spending on meaningful goals. Focus on paying off your debts strategically, starting with the ones that have the highest interest rates.

Reflect on how debt repayment fits into your overall plan. Are you making consistent progress, or do you feel stuck? Developing a clear strategy helps you regain control and free up resources for other priorities.

Automating Your Savings and Payments

Automation simplifies financial management and ensures that your priorities are addressed consistently. Set up automatic transfers to your savings account and automate bill payments to avoid late fees. This reduces the temptation to spend money before you save or pay what's due.

Reflect on how automation might help you stay on track. Would it remove stress and make financial management feel more effortless? Simplifying your routine can free up mental energy for other goals.

Changing Your Mindset

Breaking the paycheck-to-paycheck cycle isn't just about numbers—it's also about shifting your mindset. Start viewing financial challenges as opportunities to grow and improve. Celebrate small victories, like saving your first $100 or paying off a credit card, and use them as motivation to keep going.

Reflect on your relationship with money. Do you feel empowered to make changes, or does financial stress hold you back? Adopting a growth mindset can transform how you approach your finances and inspire lasting change.

Reflecting on Your Progress

Breaking the paycheck-to-paycheck cycle takes time, effort, and persistence, but every small step brings you closer to financial freedom. Reflect on the progress you've made so far, the challenges you've overcome, and the lessons you've learned along the way.

Seeking Support When Needed

When navigating financial challenges or striving to achieve ambitious goals, seeking support can be a transformative step. While the thought of asking for help might seem daunting, having the right people and organizations in your corner can ease your journey, provide clarity, and empower you to make informed decisions. Mentors, financial advisors, and community organizations offer the guidance, knowledge, and encouragement you need to thrive, no matter where you are in your financial journey.

The Power of Support

At some point, everyone faces financial hurdles that feel overwhelming. Whether it's struggling to manage debt, planning for a major life event, or simply learning how to save more effectively, these challenges can leave you feeling stuck. The key to overcoming these obstacles often lies in reaching out to those who can help.

Seeking support isn't about admitting defeat—it's about recognizing that you don't have to do everything alone. By leveraging the knowledge and experience of others, you can gain new perspectives, learn proven strategies, and build confidence in your ability to succeed. Reflect on the moments in your life when someone's advice or encouragement made a difference. How might similar support help you in your financial journey?

Defining Your Needs

Before seeking support, take a moment to assess your financial goals and challenges. Are you looking to pay off debt, build wealth, or navigate a complex situation like buying a home or saving for retirement? Identifying your needs will help you connect with the right resources and people.

For example, if you're focused on reducing debt, you might benefit from working with a financial counsellor or attending workshops offered by local nonprofits. If you're exploring investment opportunities, a financial advisor with expertise in wealth management could be a valuable ally. Reflect on your current priorities and the areas where you feel stuck. What kind of support could make the biggest difference for you right now?

Finding Mentors to Guide You

Mentors are individuals who have walked the path you're on and are willing to share their experiences, wisdom, and advice. They can offer practical insights and emotional support, helping you navigate challenges with confidence. Financial mentors, in particular, can be instrumental in teaching you about budgeting, saving, investing, and more.

When seeking a mentor, look for someone whose values and achievements align with your goals. This might be a family member who has successfully managed their finances, a friend who's started a thriving business, or a community leader who's passionate about financial education. Building a relationship with a mentor requires trust, mutual respect, and a willingness to learn.

Think about the people in your life who inspire you. Are there individuals you admire for their financial success, discipline, or creativity? Consider reaching out to them with a genuine desire to learn. Many people are happy to share their experiences when approached with sincerity and openness.

Working with Financial Advisors

Financial advisors are professionals who provide expert guidance on a range of topics, including investments, retirement planning, and tax strategies. They can help you create a personalized financial plan, identify opportunities for growth, and avoid common pitfalls.

When choosing a financial advisor, it's important to find someone you trust. Look for advisors who are certified, transparent about their fees, and committed to acting in your best interest. Consider asking friends or colleagues for recommendations, or search for advisors through professional organizations like the Financial Planning Association or the National Association of Personal Financial Advisors.

Reflect on the areas where professional advice might benefit you most. Are you planning for a major financial milestone, like buying a home or starting a business? Or are you looking for long-term strategies to build wealth and secure your future? Working with a financial advisor can provide clarity and direction, helping you make confident decisions.

Leveraging Community Organizations

Community organizations are invaluable resources for individuals and families facing financial challenges. These nonprofits, local agencies, and religious groups often offer free or low-cost services, including financial education workshops, budgeting assistance, and access to emergency funds.

For example, many organizations provide one-on-one financial counseling to help you create a budget, reduce debt, or save for specific goals. Others offer programs that address immediate needs, such as housing assistance, food support, or job training. By connecting with these resources, you can access the tools and support you need to move forward.

Reflect on the resources available in your community. Are there organizations or programs you've considered but haven't explored yet? Taking that first step could open the door to valuable opportunities and connections.

Building a Supportive Network

Your financial journey is unique, but that doesn't mean you have to face it alone. Building a network of supportive individuals and organizations creates a foundation of encouragement, accountability, and shared knowledge. This network might include mentors, advisors, community leaders, or even friends and family who share your goals.

To build your support network, start by reaching out to people you trust. Share your goals and challenges, and ask for their advice or recommendations. Attend local workshops, join online communities, or participate in events that align with your interests. These connections can provide inspiration, motivation, and practical guidance.

Reflect on your current support network. Are there individuals or groups you could lean on more often? Strengthening these relationships can enhance your ability to navigate financial challenges and achieve your goals.

Overcoming Barriers to Seeking Help

Many people hesitate to seek financial support because they fear judgment, feel ashamed of their situation, or believe they should handle everything on their own. These barriers can prevent you from accessing the help you need to succeed.

It's important to remember that everyone faces financial challenges at some point, and seeking support is a proactive step toward improvement. Mentors, advisors, and community organizations are there to help—not to judge. Reflect on any fears or misconceptions that might be holding you back. How can you reframe these thoughts to embrace the support available to you?

Taking the First Step

Reaching out for support can feel intimidating, but taking that first step is often the hardest part. Start small by having an honest conversation with someone you trust, whether it's a family member, friend, or advisor. Share your goals, ask for their perspective, and explore the resources they recommend.

Reflect on the first step you can take today. Is there a call you've been meaning to make or a conversation you've been avoiding? Taking action, even in a small way, moves you closer to the support you need.

Reflecting on the Impact of Support

Seeking support is a powerful way to accelerate your financial progress. Reflect on how guidance, encouragement, and resources have helped you in other areas of your life. What lessons can you apply to your financial goals? By embracing collaboration and expertise, you're creating a foundation for long-term success.

Chapter 11

Advocating for Fair Financial Opportunities

Closing the Wage Gap

The wage gap is a persistent issue that affects millions of women, particularly Black women, who often face greater disparities in pay. While systemic change is essential to achieve true equity, you also have the power to advocate for yourself in the workplace. Learning to negotiate salaries and fight for fair pay is not just about securing the compensation you deserve—it's about valuing your worth, breaking barriers, and paving the way for others.

Understanding the Wage Gap and Its Impact

The wage gap is the difference in earnings between groups of people based on gender, race, or ethnicity. For Black women, the statistics are particularly stark: on average, Black women earn just 63 cents for every dollar earned by a white, non-Hispanic man. This disparity accumulates over time, leading to significant losses in lifetime earnings, reduced retirement savings, and limited opportunities for wealth-building.

Reflect on how the wage gap may have impacted your own life or the lives of women you know. What opportunities might have been lost or delayed because of unfair compensation? Acknowledging these realities is the first step toward change.

Valuing Your Worth

Before you can effectively negotiate, it's important to understand and value your worth. Your skills, experience, and contributions are valuable assets that deserve fair compensation. Start by researching salaries in your field to understand what others in similar roles are earning. Websites like Glassdoor, Payscale, and LinkedIn Salary Insights can provide useful benchmarks.

Reflect on your accomplishments and unique strengths. What do you bring to the table that sets you apart? Writing these down can boost your confidence and provide concrete points to highlight during negotiations.

Preparing for Negotiation

Preparation is key to successful salary negotiations. Start by gathering data to back up your request. This includes salary benchmarks, examples of your accomplishments, and evidence of how your work has contributed to the organization's success. Being well-prepared shows that you've done your homework and makes your case more compelling.

Practice your negotiation conversation with a trusted friend, mentor, or career coach. Role-playing different scenarios can help you feel more confident and ready to handle objections or counteroffers. Reflect on how preparation could impact your confidence during the negotiation process. Are there areas where you need more clarity or support?

Overcoming Common Fears

Negotiating can feel intimidating, especially if you fear rejection or worry about being seen as demanding. It's important to remember that salary negotiation is a normal part of the employment process. Employers expect candidates to advocate for themselves, and doing so demonstrates confidence and professionalism.

Reflect on any fears or doubts that may hold you back from negotiating. Are they rooted in past experiences or cultural expectations? Challenging these fears and reframing negotiation as a skill to be practiced can help you move forward with confidence.

Crafting Your Message

When it's time to negotiate, approach the conversation with a collaborative mindset. Frame your request as a discussion about mutual benefit, focusing on how your skills and contributions align with the organization's goals. Use specific examples to demonstrate your value, such as projects you've led, revenue you've generated, or problems you've solved.

For example, instead of saying, "I need a raise," you could say, "Given my achievements over the past year, including increasing sales by 20% and streamlining processes that saved the company $15,000, I'd like to discuss aligning my compensation with the market rate for my role."

Reflect on how you can present your case in a way that feels authentic and compelling. What language feels natural to you, and how can you tailor your message to the situation?

Handling Pushback

Not every negotiation will result in an immediate "yes." Employers may push back with budget constraints, market conditions, or other reasons. While these responses can be frustrating, they don't have to end the conversation. Instead, use them as an opportunity to explore alternatives, such as performance-based raises, additional benefits, or professional development opportunities.

Reflect on how you've handled rejection or pushback in the past. Are there ways you can stay calm and persistent in the face of objections? Maintaining a professional and solution-oriented approach can keep the conversation open.

Advocating Beyond Your Own Salary

Fighting for equitable pay isn't just about your own compensation—it's also about creating a culture of fairness and transparency in the workplace. This might involve mentoring others, sharing resources, or advocating for company-wide pay audits and equity initiatives. By speaking up, you can help break down systemic barriers and ensure that others don't face the same challenges.

Reflect on how you can use your voice and influence to advocate for broader change. Are there initiatives you could support or conversations you could start to promote equity in your organization?

Celebrating Your Wins

Negotiating and advocating for equitable pay is no small feat, and every victory deserves to be celebrated. Whether you secure a raise, gain valuable experience in the process, or open the door to future opportunities, each step forward is an achievement worth acknowledging.

Reflect on your journey and the progress you've made. How has advocating for yourself changed your perspective or boosted your confidence? Recognizing your growth reinforces your ability to keep pushing for what you deserve.

Reflecting on the Bigger Picture

Closing the wage gap requires collective action, systemic change, and individual advocacy. By valuing your worth, preparing for negotiations, and advocating for fairness, you're contributing to a larger movement toward equity and justice. Reflect on how your efforts can inspire and empower others. You have the power to create change—not just for yourself, but for future generations.

Financial Rights and Protections

Financial discrimination can take many forms, from unequal pay and biased lending practices to systemic barriers that make it harder for certain groups to access opportunities. Understanding your financial rights and the laws designed to protect you is a crucial step toward empowerment. It equips you with the tools to advocate for fairness, challenge discriminatory practices, and create a more equitable future for yourself and your community.

Why Financial Rights Matter

Your financial rights are fundamental to your ability to thrive. These rights ensure that you can participate fully in the economy, access resources fairly, and pursue opportunities without facing barriers based on your identity. Discrimination, whether overt or subtle, can have lasting impacts on your financial stability, but knowing your rights helps you push back against injustice.

Reflect on your own experiences with financial systems. Have there been moments when you felt unfairly treated or excluded? Recognizing these patterns is the first step toward addressing them.

Key Laws Protecting Against Financial Discrimination

Several laws exist to protect individuals from financial discrimination, ensuring equal access to resources and opportunities. While these laws are not perfect, they provide a framework for holding institutions accountable.

The Equal Pay Act of 1963 mandates that men and women receive equal pay for equal work. Despite this, pay disparities persist, particularly for Black women and women of color. Knowing your rights under this act empowers you to challenge inequities in compensation.

The Civil Rights Act of 1964 prohibits discrimination in employment, including hiring, promotion, and pay practices, based on race, color, religion, sex, or national origin. This law is foundational in protecting workers from systemic biases that limit their opportunities.

The Fair Housing Act of 1968 prevents discrimination in housing-related transactions, including renting, buying, or securing a mortgage. This law aims to ensure that all individuals have equal access to housing opportunities, regardless of their background.

The Equal Credit Opportunity Act of 1974 ensures that lenders cannot discriminate based on race, color, religion, national origin, sex, marital status, or age. It's a critical protection for individuals seeking credit for homes, businesses, or personal needs.

The Lilly Ledbetter Fair Pay Act of 2009 strengthens protections against pay discrimination by extending the time frame in which employees can file claims. This law recognizes that discriminatory practices are often revealed over time and gives workers more opportunities to seek justice.

Reflect on how these laws intersect with your financial experiences. Are there protections you weren't aware of? Understanding these frameworks empowers you to take action if your rights are violated.

Recognizing Discrimination

Discrimination in financial systems isn't always blatant. It often shows up in subtle ways, such as being offered less favorable loan terms, being denied opportunities without clear justification, or being excluded from conversations about advancement. Learning to recognize these patterns is key to advocating for yourself.

Reflect on any instances where you've felt treated unfairly in financial matters. Were there red flags or inconsistencies that stood out to you? Trusting your instincts and seeking advice can help you navigate these situations.

Resources for Financial Protection

If you believe your financial rights have been violated, there are resources available to help you seek justice. Government agencies like the Equal Employment Opportunity Commission (EEOC) and the Consumer Financial Protection Bureau (CFPB) investigate claims of discrimination and provide guidance on next steps.

Nonprofit organizations and advocacy groups, such as the National Women's Law Center and the NAACP Legal Defense Fund, also offer support for individuals facing financial discrimination. These organizations can connect you with legal resources, educational materials, and community networks.

Reflect on how accessing these resources could strengthen your ability to advocate for fairness. Are there groups or agencies you could reach out to for guidance or support?

Taking Action Against Discrimination

If you experience financial discrimination, taking action can feel daunting, but it's an important step toward change. Start by documenting the situation thoroughly. Keep records of emails, conversations, and any relevant documents that support your case. This evidence will be critical if you decide to file a complaint or pursue legal action.

Consider seeking legal advice from a trusted attorney or organization that specializes in financial rights. They can help you understand your options and navigate the process of filing complaints or lawsuits.

Reflect on how taking action could impact your financial future and the broader fight for equity. Are there ways you can use your experience to inspire change or support others facing similar challenges?

Empowering Your Community

Understanding your financial rights isn't just about protecting yourself—it's also about empowering your community. Sharing knowledge, advocating for policy changes, and supporting initiatives that promote fairness help create a more equitable system for everyone.

Reflect on how you can contribute to this collective effort. Are there opportunities to mentor others, participate in advocacy campaigns, or educate your peers about their rights? Every action you take strengthens the fight for justice.

Reflecting on Your Journey

Navigating financial systems can be challenging, especially when discrimination creates additional barriers. But by understanding your rights, seeking support, and taking action when necessary, you're building a foundation of resilience and empowerment. Reflect on how far you've come and the progress you've made. What lessons have you learned, and how can you continue to advocate for fairness in your financial life?

Leveraging Collective Power

Collective power has always been a driving force in shaping history, fostering change, and creating opportunities. For Black women, who have faced systemic barriers in accessing financial resources and opportunities, leveraging collective power is not only a strategy for survival but a transformative tool for building lasting wealth, stability, and equity. Supporting Black women-led financial initiatives and advocacy groups is about recognizing the unique challenges faced by Black women while amplifying their leadership and solutions. It's about coming together to build a future where fairness and opportunity are the norm, not the exception.

The Foundation of Collective Power

Collective power is rooted in the belief that we are stronger together. For centuries, Black women have demonstrated the power of unity through mutual aid societies, grassroots movements, and community-based financial models. These efforts have provided resources, education, and support in times when traditional systems excluded or marginalized them. Today, this legacy continues through initiatives that prioritize financial empowerment, advocacy, and community growth.

Reflect on the times you've witnessed or experienced the strength of collective power. How has being part of a group or community shaped your ability to overcome challenges? These moments are a reminder of what can be achieved when people come together with a shared purpose.

Supporting Black Women-Led Financial Initiatives

Black women-led financial initiatives address critical gaps in access to funding, education, and economic opportunities. These organizations are often born out of necessity, designed to address the systemic barriers that make it harder for Black women to thrive financially. Supporting these initiatives is about more than just financial contributions—it's about amplifying their impact, spreading awareness, and ensuring their sustainability.

For example, initiatives like *Black Girl Ventures* and *The Women's Center for Economic Empowerment* focus on empowering Black women entrepreneurs through funding, mentorship, and resources. Programs like these help bridge the gap between ambition and opportunity, enabling Black women to build businesses that create jobs, support families, and uplift communities.

Reflect on how you can contribute to these efforts. Are there organizations in your community or online that align with your values and goals? Whether it's through donations, volunteering, or simply spreading the word, every action makes a difference.

Investing in Black-Owned Businesses

Investing in Black-owned businesses is one of the most direct ways to support collective economic empowerment. These businesses are often hubs of innovation, creativity, and community support, but they frequently face challenges like limited access to capital and discriminatory lending practices. By intentionally choosing to support Black-owned businesses, you're contributing to their growth and sustainability.

Consider incorporating Black-owned businesses into your daily life. This might mean buying products or services from Black-owned companies, promoting them within your network, or even investing in their growth through equity crowdfunding or venture capital.

Reflect on your current spending habits. Are there ways to shift your purchases toward Black-owned businesses or brands? Small changes in where you spend your money can have a ripple effect, strengthening the financial foundation of entire communities.

Building Financial Literacy Collectively

Financial literacy is a cornerstone of empowerment, but it's often inaccessible to those who need it most. Black women-led initiatives that focus on financial education play a crucial role in closing this gap, offering workshops, resources, and mentorship programs that demystify money management and wealth-building strategies.

Organizations like *The Black Women's Wealth Alliance* and *My Fab Finance* specialize in providing culturally relevant financial education that addresses the unique experiences of Black women. These programs empower participants to take control of their finances, set goals, and build generational wealth.

Reflect on your own financial knowledge. Are there areas where you could benefit from additional education or resources? Sharing these tools with others strengthens collective financial empowerment and ensures that no one is left behind.

Advocacy for Policy Change

Systemic change requires advocacy. Black women-led advocacy groups work tirelessly to address policies that perpetuate financial inequality, from the racial wealth gap to predatory lending practices. Supporting these efforts means standing behind initiatives that fight for fair treatment, equitable access, and economic justice.

For instance, *The Black Women's Roundtable* advocates for policies that promote economic equity, while *The National Coalition on Black Civic*

Participation focuses on increasing access to voting and representation, which directly impacts economic opportunities. By supporting these organizations, you're amplifying their ability to create systemic change.

Reflect on the policies or issues that resonate most with you. Are there opportunities to get involved in advocacy efforts, attend events, or support campaigns? Advocacy is a powerful way to leverage collective power for lasting impact.

Mentorship as a Tool for Empowerment

Mentorship is a form of collective power that builds bridges between experience and ambition. By mentoring others, you're not just sharing knowledge—you're creating a pipeline of future leaders who will continue to advocate for and uplift their communities. Mentorship also fosters a sense of belonging and confidence, helping mentees navigate challenges and seize opportunities.

Reflect on your own experiences with mentorship. Have you benefited from the guidance of a mentor, or is there someone you've supported along their journey? Consider how you can contribute to the cycle of empowerment by offering your time, expertise, or encouragement to others.

Collaborating for Greater Impact

Collaboration amplifies the efforts of individuals and organizations. Black women-led financial initiatives often partner with other groups, businesses, and institutions to expand their reach and resources. Whether it's through joint events, shared funding opportunities, or collective advocacy, these collaborations demonstrate the strength of unity.

Reflect on how collaboration could enhance your efforts to support collective power. Are there opportunities to work with others, join networks, or contribute to shared goals? Building partnerships creates a multiplier effect that benefits everyone involved.

Celebrating Achievements and Progress

Acknowledging and celebrating the achievements of Black women-led financial initiatives is an important part of leveraging collective power. Whether it's a new business launch, a successful policy change, or a milestone in community impact, these moments deserve recognition. Celebrations not only inspire others to join the movement but also reinforce the value of the work being done.

Reflect on the successes you've witnessed or been part of. How can you share these stories to inspire others and amplify their impact? Celebrating progress builds momentum and strengthens the sense of community.

Reflecting on Your Role in Collective Power

Leveraging collective power starts with recognizing your ability to contribute. Whether it's through financial support, advocacy, mentorship, or collaboration, your actions have the potential to make a difference. Reflect on the unique skills, resources, and perspectives you bring to the table. How can you use them to uplift others and drive meaningful change?

Chapter 12

Building Wealth Beyond Saving

Turning Savings into Investments

Saving is the foundation of financial stability, but investing is the key to building wealth. While savings offer security and liquidity, investments create opportunities for growth and long-term prosperity. Transforming your hard-earned savings into investments can feel intimidating, but with knowledge, strategy, and a willingness to take calculated risks, you can create a financial future that reflects your goals and dreams.

The Power of Investing

When you invest, you're putting your money to work for you. Unlike savings, which typically grow slowly through modest interest rates, investments have the potential to multiply your wealth significantly over time. Whether through real estate, entrepreneurship, or the stock market, investing allows you to leverage your resources for higher returns, giving you the ability to achieve financial goals faster.

Reflect on the idea of your money working for you. How does it feel to think of your savings as a tool for creating opportunities? Shifting your perspective in this way is the first step toward confident investing.

Real Estate: Building Wealth Through Property

Real estate has long been considered one of the most reliable ways to grow wealth. Owning property offers multiple avenues for financial gain, including rental income, property appreciation, and tax advantages. It also provides a tangible asset that can be passed down to future generations.

Starting Small with Real Estate Investments

If you're new to real estate, consider starting with a small, manageable investment. This might be purchasing your first home, investing in a rental property, or exploring real estate crowdfunding platforms that allow you to invest in properties with a lower upfront cost. These options provide entry points to the market without requiring significant capital.

Reflect on your current financial position. Could real estate fit into your investment strategy, even on a small scale? Starting modestly allows you to gain experience and confidence in the real estate market.

Maximizing Rental Income

Owning rental properties can create a steady stream of income while your asset appreciates over time. To succeed, it's essential to research local rental markets, choose properties in desirable locations, and calculate potential expenses like maintenance, taxes, and property management fees. Reflect on the areas in your community that might offer strong rental opportunities. Are there neighborhoods experiencing growth or demand that you could explore further?

Flipping Properties for Profit

For those willing to take on more risk and effort, flipping properties—buying undervalued homes, renovating them, and selling them for a profit—can be a lucrative strategy. This approach requires a keen eye for market trends, budgeting skills, and a network of reliable contractors. Reflect on your comfort level with hands-on projects and your ability to manage the complexities of flipping properties. Could this be an avenue that aligns with your skills and interests?

Entrepreneurship: Turning Ideas into Income

Entrepreneurship is another powerful way to grow wealth, offering both financial rewards and the fulfillment of building something uniquely your own. Whether you're launching a small side hustle or scaling a larger business, entrepreneurship allows you to leverage your skills, passions, and creativity to generate income and create opportunities for others.

Identifying Your Niche

Successful businesses often start with identifying a need or problem that you can solve. Reflect on your own experiences, skills, and interests. Are there gaps in the market that you're uniquely positioned to address? Whether it's a product, service, or innovative solution, your idea could become the foundation of a thriving business.

Starting Small and Scaling Gradually

You don't need a large investment to begin your entrepreneurial journey. Many successful businesses start as side hustles, allowing you to test ideas, build a customer base, and refine your approach before committing fully. Reflect on any hobbies or skills you could monetize on a small scale. Could these activities grow into a sustainable business with time and effort?

Leveraging Technology and Networks

Today's technology makes it easier than ever to launch and grow a business. From e-commerce platforms to social media marketing tools, there are countless resources available to help you reach your audience and streamline operations. Reflect on how you can use technology to amplify your efforts and connect with potential customers. Are there online communities or networks you could tap into for support and inspiration?

Building a Legacy Through Entrepreneurship

Beyond financial rewards, entrepreneurship allows you to create a legacy of innovation and opportunity. By building a successful business, you're contributing to your community, creating jobs, and inspiring others to pursue their dreams. Reflect on the impact you want your business to have. How can your entrepreneurial journey align with your values and contribute to the greater good?

The Stock Market: Harnessing the Power of Compounding

The stock market offers one of the most accessible and effective ways to grow your wealth. By investing in stocks, bonds, mutual funds, or exchange-traded funds (ETFs), you're participating in the growth of companies and economies around the world. Over time, the power of compounding—earning returns on both your initial investment and previous gains—can lead to significant wealth accumulation.

Getting Started in the Stock Market

If you're new to investing, the stock market can feel overwhelming. Start by educating yourself on basic concepts like stocks, dividends, and risk tolerance. Reflect on your financial goals and timeline. Are you investing for long-term growth, retirement, or specific milestones? Understanding your objectives helps you choose investments that align with your needs.

Diversifying Your Portfolio

Diversification is key to managing risk in the stock market. By spreading your investments across different asset classes, industries, and regions, you reduce the impact of any single loss. Reflect on how diversification could enhance your investment strategy. Are there areas where you could broaden your portfolio to balance risk and reward?

Leveraging Index Funds and ETFs

For many investors, index funds and ETFs offer a simple, low-cost way to gain exposure to the stock market. These funds track the performance of a specific market index, such as the S&P 500, and provide instant diversification. Reflect on whether these options could fit into your investment plan. Could they simplify your approach while providing steady, long-term growth?

Staying the Course During Market Volatility

The stock market is known for its ups and downs, and staying invested during periods of volatility can be challenging. Reflect on your risk tolerance and ability to remain patient during market fluctuations. Are there strategies you could adopt, such as dollar-cost averaging, to stay consistent with your investments?

Reflecting on Your Investment Journey

Turning savings into investments is a powerful step toward building wealth, but it requires knowledge, strategy, and persistence. Reflect on the opportunities that resonate most with you—whether it's real estate, entrepreneurship, or the stock market—and consider how they align with your financial goals and values.

Side Hustles for Extra Income

Building wealth isn't always about cutting back—it's also about finding ways to earn more. Side hustles, or secondary income streams, offer an excellent opportunity to supplement your primary income, accelerate your savings, and explore your passions. With the right approach, a side hustle can go from being a temporary boost to a consistent source of financial empowerment. Whether you're saving for a specific goal, paying down debt, or building long-term wealth, side hustles provide the flexibility to make your financial dreams more attainable.

Why Side Hustles Are Worth Exploring

Side hustles aren't just about making extra money; they're about taking control of your financial future. For many, a side hustle represents freedom—the freedom to create a safety net, fund goals, or even transition into a new career. It allows you to diversify your income streams, reducing your reliance on a single paycheck and providing financial security.

Reflect on how a side hustle could fit into your life. Are there specific goals or challenges that an additional income stream could help you address? Identifying your "why" gives you a clear sense of purpose as you explore opportunities.

Identifying Your Strengths and Interests

The most successful side hustles often align with your skills, interests, and values. When you enjoy what you're doing, it feels less like work and more like an extension of your passions. Take some time to reflect on what you're good at and what you love to do. Do you have skills in writing, design, teaching, or crafting? Are there hobbies you could monetize, like baking, photography, or fitness?

Reflect on the activities that bring you joy and fulfillment. Could these become income-generating opportunities? When your side hustle aligns with your strengths, it feels rewarding both financially and personally.

Exploring Flexible Opportunities

Side hustles are as diverse as the people who pursue them. The key is finding one that fits your schedule, interests, and income goals. Let's explore some popular options:

Freelancing and Consulting

If you have expertise in a specific area, freelancing or consulting can be a lucrative side hustle. Whether it's writing, graphic design, marketing, or IT support, offering your services on platforms like Upwork, Fiverr, or LinkedIn allows you to connect with clients who value your skills.

Reflect on your professional experience. Are there skills you've honed in your career that could be translated into freelance work? Offering your expertise on your own terms can be both empowering and profitable.

E-Commerce and Online Selling

The rise of online marketplaces like Etsy, eBay, and Shopify has made it easier than ever to sell products. Whether you're creating handmade items, reselling vintage finds, or curating niche products, e-commerce offers a flexible way to earn income.

Reflect on whether you have products or ideas that could appeal to a specific audience. Do you have a talent for crafting, sourcing unique items, or identifying trends? E-commerce could be a great fit for you.

Teaching and Tutoring

If you have a talent for explaining concepts or a passion for a particular subject, teaching or tutoring can be a fulfilling side hustle. Platforms like VIPKid, Wyzant, and Skillshare allow you to connect with students, share your knowledge, and earn income.

Reflect on your areas of expertise. Could you teach a language, tutor in math or science, or offer lessons in music or art? Sharing your skills with others can be both rewarding and lucrative.

Driving and Delivery Services

For those who prefer flexible, on-the-go work, driving for rideshare services like Uber or delivering for companies like DoorDash and Instacart can provide steady income. These options allow you to set your own schedule and earn money while exploring your city.

Reflect on whether these opportunities align with your availability and lifestyle. Are you comfortable interacting with customers and managing your time independently? If so, this type of work could be a practical choice.

Balancing a Side Hustle with Your Life

Adding a side hustle to your routine requires careful planning to ensure it doesn't overwhelm you. The goal is to enhance your financial situation, not to burn yourself out. Start by setting clear boundaries for how much time and energy you're willing to dedicate to your side hustle. This might mean working a few hours each evening or dedicating weekends to your new venture.

Reflect on your current schedule and responsibilities. How much time could you realistically allocate to a side hustle without sacrificing your well-being or other priorities? Establishing boundaries helps you stay focused and maintain balance.

Turning Your Side Hustle Into a Business

For some, a side hustle is just the beginning. With dedication and growth, your side hustle could evolve into a full-fledged business. This transition often happens naturally as you gain experience, build a customer base, and identify opportunities for expansion.

Reflect on whether you see your side hustle as a short-term project or a potential long-term venture. Are there ways to scale your efforts, reach more customers, or diversify your offerings? Thinking strategically about growth helps you plan for the future.

Using Side Hustle Income Strategically

One of the biggest advantages of a side hustle is the freedom to decide how to use the extra income. Whether you're paying down debt, building an emergency fund, or investing in your future, the money you earn can accelerate your progress toward financial goals.

Reflect on your financial priorities. How could your side hustle income make the biggest impact on your overall financial health? Having a clear plan for your earnings ensures that your hard work translates into meaningful results.

Overcoming Challenges and Staying Motivated

Like any venture, side hustles come with their own set of challenges. From finding clients to managing your time effectively, there will be obstacles to navigate. Staying motivated requires a clear understanding of why you started and what you hope to achieve.

Reflect on the challenges you've faced in other areas of your life. How did you overcome them, and what lessons can you apply to your side hustle? Building resilience and staying focused on your goals will keep you moving forward.

Reflecting on Your Side Hustle Journey

Every side hustle journey is unique, shaped by your goals, passions, and efforts. Reflect on how far you've come, the lessons you've learned, and the impact your side hustle has had on your financial life. Whether it's a small step or a major leap, every success deserves to be celebrated.

From Saver to Investor

Saving is an essential step toward financial security, but investing is what propels you into the realm of long-term wealth. It's a shift from simply holding onto money to actively making it grow. Moving from a saver's mindset to an investor's requires understanding the power of investing, building confidence in your abilities, and taking deliberate steps toward turning your financial goals into reality. This transition is not just about numbers—it's about embracing the possibilities that come with creating a legacy of financial empowerment.

Understanding the Difference Between Saving and Investing

Saving is about protecting your money. It's the act of putting funds aside in a secure place, such as a savings account, for future use. While saving offers safety and liquidity, it often grows slowly due to low-interest rates, particularly when inflation is factored in.

Investing, on the other hand, is about growing your money. When you invest, you put your funds into assets like stocks, bonds, or real estate, with the expectation of earning returns over time. While investments carry risks, they also offer significantly higher growth potential compared to savings.

Reflect on your current financial habits. Are you focused primarily on saving, or have you started exploring investment opportunities? Understanding where you are now is the first step toward building a strategy for long-term wealth.

Overcoming the Fear of Investing

For many first-time investors, the idea of putting money into the market feels risky or intimidating. Concerns about losing money, not knowing where to start, or feeling out of your depth are common barriers. The key to overcoming these fears is education and preparation.

Investing doesn't have to be complicated or overwhelming. Start by learning the basics, such as the difference between stocks and bonds, how mutual funds and ETFs work, and the concept of risk versus reward. Knowledge is a powerful antidote to fear.

Reflect on the fears or doubts you may have about investing. Are they based on past experiences, misinformation, or a lack of understanding? Taking the time to educate yourself can transform these fears into confidence.

Building an Investor's Mindset

Becoming an investor isn't just about the technical aspects of choosing assets—it's about adopting a mindset of growth and opportunity. An investor's mindset focuses on the long term, recognizing that wealth-building is a journey that requires patience, persistence, and a willingness to take calculated risks.

An important part of this mindset is understanding the concept of delayed gratification. Investing often means putting money toward future gains rather than immediate rewards. Reflect on how you view the trade-off between short-term spending and long-term wealth. Are there adjustments you could make to prioritize your future self?

Starting Small and Staying Consistent

One of the biggest misconceptions about investing is that you need a lot of money to get started. In reality, many investment platforms allow you to begin with small amounts, making it accessible to almost anyone. The key is to start where you are and build momentum over time.

Consistency is more important than size when it comes to investing. By contributing regularly to your investment accounts, even in small amounts, you harness the power of compounding, where your earnings generate additional returns over time.

Reflect on your current savings habits. Could you redirect a portion of your monthly savings toward an investment account? Starting small helps you build confidence and create a habit that leads to long-term growth.

Exploring Different Types of Investments

Investing offers a wide range of options to suit different goals, risk tolerances, and timelines. Here's an overview of some common investment types:

Stocks: Owning shares in a company gives you a stake in its success. Stocks offer high growth potential but come with greater risk.

Bonds: Bonds are essentially loans you make to governments or corporations, providing steady income with lower risk than stocks.

Mutual Funds and ETFs: These investment vehicles pool money from multiple investors to buy a diversified portfolio of assets, offering simplicity and diversification.

Real Estate: Investing in property can provide rental income and long-term appreciation, though it often requires a larger initial investment.

Retirement Accounts: Tax-advantaged accounts like 401(k)s or IRAs are designed to help you save for retirement while benefiting from compounding over decades.

Reflect on which investment options resonate most with you. Are there types of investments that align with your goals and risk tolerance? Starting with one or two options helps you gain experience without feeling overwhelmed.

Staying Focused on the Long Term

Investing is a marathon, not a sprint. Markets will have ups and downs, and it's natural to feel uneasy during periods of volatility. However, staying focused on your long-term goals helps you ride out short-term fluctuations and avoid making impulsive decisions.

Reflect on your ability to stay patient and focused when faced with uncertainty. Are there strategies you could adopt, like setting clear goals or working with a financial advisor, to help you stay on track?

The Role of Diversification

Diversification is a key principle of investing that involves spreading your money across different types of assets to reduce risk. By not putting all your eggs in one basket, you protect your portfolio from significant losses if one investment underperforms.

Reflect on how diversification could strengthen your investment strategy. Are there areas where you could broaden your portfolio to balance risk and reward?

Building Confidence Through Education

The more you learn about investing, the more confident you'll feel in your ability to make informed decisions. Consider reading books, attending workshops, or taking online courses to deepen your understanding of financial markets and strategies.

Reflect on the resources available to you. Are there books, mentors, or programs that could help you build your investment knowledge? Investing in your education is one of the best ways to set yourself up for success.

Creating a Legacy Through Investing

Investing isn't just about personal gain—it's also about creating opportunities for your family and community. By building wealth, you're setting the stage for future generations to thrive and contributing to a legacy of empowerment and progress.

Reflect on the impact you want your investments to have. Are there ways to align your financial goals with your values and create a lasting legacy?

Reflecting on Your Progress

The journey from saver to investor is one of growth, learning, and transformation. Reflect on how far you've come, the steps you've taken, and the progress you've made. Every decision you make to invest in your future brings you closer to financial freedom and the life you envision.

Chapter 13

Celebrating Milestones and Staying Motivated

Tracking Your Progress

When you set out on a savings journey, it's easy to focus so much on the destination that you overlook the strides you've already made. Tracking your progress isn't just about numbers; it's about celebrating how far you've come, identifying areas for improvement, and staying motivated to keep going. By using the right tools and techniques, you can gain clarity, maintain focus, and build confidence in your ability to achieve your financial goals.

The Importance of Tracking Progress

Your financial journey is just that—a journey. Without a way to measure progress, it's easy to feel lost or discouraged, especially when challenges arise. Tracking provides tangible evidence of your efforts and allows you to see the bigger picture. Whether you're saving for an emergency fund, paying off debt, or working toward a long-term goal like homeownership, tracking your progress reminds you that each small step is moving you closer to success.

Reflect on how you currently measure your savings efforts. Do you rely on mental notes, or do you use tools to keep track? A structured approach can help you feel more in control and motivated to stay on course.

Choosing the Right Tools for Tracking

There's no one-size-fits-all solution for tracking your savings journey. The right tools depend on your preferences, goals, and financial habits.

Some people prefer the simplicity of pen and paper, while others thrive with the automation and insights provided by apps or software.

Savings Trackers and Journals

A dedicated savings tracker or journal is a simple yet powerful way to monitor your progress. You can create your own system using a notebook or printable templates, or purchase a pre-designed savings journal. These tools allow you to record your goals, track contributions, and reflect on milestones.

Reflect on whether a physical tracker aligns with your personality and habits. Do you enjoy the act of writing things down and seeing your progress in a tangible way? This method can be especially satisfying for visual learners and those who find joy in documenting their journey.

Budgeting and Financial Apps

For those who prefer a digital approach, budgeting and savings apps offer convenience and real-time tracking. Apps like Mint, YNAB (You Need A Budget), or EveryDollar allow you to connect your accounts, set goals, and receive updates on your progress. Many apps also provide insights into your spending habits, helping you identify areas where you can save more.

Reflect on how technology fits into your financial routine. Are you comfortable using apps to manage your finances? If so, these tools can streamline your efforts and provide valuable insights at the touch of a button.

Spreadsheets for Customization

If you enjoy a more hands-on approach, creating a custom spreadsheet can be an excellent way to track your savings. Programs like Microsoft Excel or Google Sheets allow you to design a system tailored to your needs. You can include columns for income, expenses, savings contributions, and goals, and use formulas to calculate totals and progress.

Reflect on your comfort level with spreadsheets. Are you willing to invest time in setting up a personalized system? This option provides flexibility and control, making it ideal for those who like to dig into the details.

Setting Clear Goals

Tracking progress starts with setting clear, specific goals. Without a target, it's difficult to measure how far you've come or determine what adjustments are needed. Whether your goal is to save $1,000 for an emergency fund, pay off a $10,000 credit card balance, or invest $5,000 in a retirement account, having a defined objective gives you something to work toward.

Reflect on the goals you've set for yourself. Are they specific, measurable, and realistic? If not, take some time to refine them so they provide a clear roadmap for your efforts.

Breaking Goals into Milestones

Large goals can feel overwhelming, but breaking them into smaller milestones makes them more manageable and rewarding. For example, if your goal is to save $5,000, you might set milestones at $1,000, $2,500, and $4,000. Each milestone represents a step closer to your ultimate goal and gives you an opportunity to celebrate your progress.

Reflect on how milestones could make your goals feel more achievable. Are there natural checkpoints within your larger objectives that you can use to mark your progress? Celebrating these moments keeps you motivated and focused.

Monitoring Contributions and Growth

Tracking your savings contributions is essential, but don't forget to monitor the growth of your accounts as well. For example, if you're saving in a high-yield savings account, compound interest may contribute to your progress over time. Similarly, investments in a retirement account or brokerage account may grow due to market performance.

Reflect on how your savings are working for you. Are there opportunities to maximize growth by choosing higher-yield options or automating contributions? Monitoring both contributions and growth ensures you're making the most of your efforts.

Reflecting on Spending Habits

Tracking progress isn't just about watching your savings grow—it's also about understanding your spending habits and how they impact your ability to save. By reviewing your expenses regularly, you can identify patterns, spot areas where you're overspending, and make adjustments to free up more money for your goals.

Reflect on your spending over the past month or year. Are there categories where you could cut back or make more intentional choices? Small changes in spending can have a big impact on your ability to save.

Staying Consistent with Your Tracking

Consistency is key to effective tracking. Whether you check your progress weekly, biweekly, or monthly, creating a routine ensures that you stay informed and engaged with your goals. Regular check-ins also give you the opportunity to adjust your approach if needed, keeping you on track even when circumstances change.

Reflect on how often you currently review your savings. Could you benefit from setting a regular schedule for tracking your progress? Consistency builds accountability and helps you maintain momentum.

Celebrating Wins Along the Way

Tracking progress isn't just about identifying what's left to do—it's also about celebrating what you've already accomplished. Each time you hit a milestone, take a moment to acknowledge your hard work and dedication. Celebrating these wins reinforces positive habits and keeps you motivated to keep going.

Reflect on how you celebrate your achievements. Are there ways to make these moments more meaningful or enjoyable? Recognizing your progress is an important part of staying inspired.

Reflecting on Your Journey

As you track your progress, take time to reflect on your journey as a whole. What have you learned about yourself and your financial habits? How has your mindset evolved, and what challenges have you overcome? These reflections provide valuable insights that can guide you as you continue working toward your goals.

Rewarding Yourself Along the Way

Achieving financial goals takes hard work, discipline, and patience. Along the way, it's important to celebrate your milestones, not only to acknowledge your progress but also to keep yourself motivated. Rewards provide a psychological boost, making the journey feel less restrictive and more sustainable. However, the key to celebrating successfully is finding a balance—one where you recognize your efforts without undermining your long-term goals.

Why Celebrating Matters

Celebration is an essential part of any journey. It acknowledges your progress, validates your hard work, and gives you the energy to keep moving forward. Without taking time to appreciate how far you've come, it's easy to feel burnt out or disconnected from the purpose behind your goals. Celebrations create positive reinforcement, encouraging you to stick with the habits and behaviors that have brought you success.

Reflect on your own milestones, whether they're financial or personal. How often do you pause to celebrate your achievements? Giving yourself permission to enjoy these moments can reignite your passion and commitment to your goals.

Defining What Celebration Looks Like for You

Celebration doesn't have to mean spending a lot of money or indulging in something extravagant. It's about choosing rewards that feel meaningful and aligned with your values. For some, that might mean enjoying a night out with friends, while for others, it could be as simple as taking a day off to relax and recharge.

Reflect on what brings you joy and satisfaction. Are there experiences or activities that make you feel rewarded without compromising your financial progress? Tailoring your celebrations to what truly matters to you ensures they remain both fulfilling and sustainable.

Setting Celebration Milestones

One of the most effective ways to incorporate rewards into your financial journey is by tying them to specific milestones. For example, if your goal is to save $10,000, you might plan a small reward for every $2,000 saved. These milestones give you something to look forward to, breaking down larger goals into manageable and motivating steps.

Reflect on how milestones could make your goals feel more achievable. Are there natural points along your journey where a celebration would feel especially meaningful? Planning these moments in advance helps you stay focused and excited.

Balancing Rewards with Responsibility

Celebrating doesn't mean throwing caution to the wind or overspending in a way that undoes your progress. The key is to strike a balance between enjoying your rewards and staying true to your goals. One approach is to allocate a small percentage of your budget specifically for celebrations. This way, you can indulge guilt-free, knowing it's part of your overall plan.

Reflect on your current approach to treating yourself. Are there ways to make your rewards more intentional and aligned with your financial priorities? A balanced approach ensures that celebrations enhance your journey rather than detract from it.

Creative and Cost-Effective Ways to Celebrate

Celebrations don't have to be expensive to be meaningful. There are countless ways to reward yourself that feel special without breaking the bank. For example, you could:

- Host a potluck dinner with friends to mark a milestone.
- Treat yourself to a favorite book, movie, or activity.
- Take a day trip to explore a new place or enjoy nature.

Reflect on the types of experiences that make you feel happiest. Are there low-cost or no-cost options that would feel equally rewarding? Being creative with your celebrations allows you to stay on track financially while still enjoying the journey.

Using Rewards to Reinforce Positive Habits

Celebrations can also serve as a way to reinforce the habits that have helped you succeed. For instance, if you've been consistent with meal prepping to save money, your reward could be a special dinner at a restaurant you've been wanting to try. This ties your celebration directly to the behavior you want to maintain, creating a positive feedback loop.

Reflect on the habits that have contributed most to your progress. Are there ways to connect your rewards to these actions, making them even more meaningful? Reinforcing good habits ensures that your progress is sustainable over the long term.

Sharing Your Success with Others

Celebrating milestones can also be an opportunity to connect with loved ones and share your success. Whether it's a family dinner, a group outing, or simply telling someone about your achievement, involving others in your celebrations can make them feel even more special. It also inspires and motivates those around you, creating a ripple effect of positivity.

Reflect on how sharing your achievements could enhance your celebrations. Are there people in your life who would love to celebrate with you and support your journey? Building a sense of community around your goals makes the process more enjoyable and rewarding.

Staying Grounded in Your Purpose

While celebrations are important, it's equally important to stay grounded in the bigger picture. Each milestone and reward is a step toward your ultimate goal, not an endpoint. Reflecting on your "why" ensures that your celebrations remain aligned with your values and purpose.

Reflect on the reasons behind your financial goals. How do your rewards connect to the life you're working to build? Staying focused on your purpose ensures that celebrations feel intentional and meaningful.

Reflecting on Your Journey

As you celebrate milestones, take time to reflect on your journey as a whole. What challenges have you overcome? What lessons have you learned? These reflections not only deepen your appreciation for your progress but also provide valuable insights for the road ahead.

Reflect on the moments that have been most significant in your journey. How have your celebrations helped you stay motivated and connected to your goals? Each milestone is a testament to your hard work and determination.

Staying Inspired Through Challenges

Life is filled with unexpected twists and turns, and your financial journey is no exception. Challenges will arise—some minor, some significant—but the key to success lies in your ability to stay inspired and motivated despite the obstacles. Building resilience, finding encouragement, and reconnecting with your purpose can help you push forward, even when the path seems steep.

Understanding the Nature of Challenges

Challenges are a natural part of growth. They test your limits, stretch your comfort zone, and often provide the greatest opportunities for learning and self-discovery. While it's normal to feel frustrated or disheartened when difficulties arise, remembering that these moments are temporary can help you regain perspective. Reflect on previous challenges you've faced and overcome. What lessons did those experiences teach you? Drawing on your past resilience can remind you of your strength and ability to persist.

Reconnecting with Your "Why"

When the going gets tough, revisiting your purpose can provide the clarity and motivation you need to keep moving forward. Your financial goals aren't just about numbers—they're about creating a life that aligns with your values, dreams, and priorities. Whether it's providing security for your family, pursuing a passion, or building a legacy, your "why" is the foundation that drives your actions.

Take a moment to reflect on your reasons for setting these goals. What inspired you to start this journey? Visualizing the future you're working toward can reignite your determination and remind you that every step, no matter how small, brings you closer to that vision.

Breaking Challenges Into Manageable Steps

When faced with a daunting obstacle, it's easy to feel overwhelmed. Breaking the challenge into smaller, more manageable steps can make it feel less intimidating and help you regain a sense of control. For example, if unexpected expenses threaten your savings, focus on one solution at a time—cutting non-essential costs, adjusting your budget, or finding temporary income sources.

Reflect on the specific challenges you're currently facing. Are there smaller actions you can take today to begin addressing them? Focusing on what's within your control helps you move forward with confidence.

Embracing Flexibility and Adaptability

Flexibility is one of the most powerful tools you can develop in your financial journey. Life rarely goes exactly as planned, and being able to adapt to changing circumstances is essential for long-term success. This might mean revising your timeline, adjusting your goals, or finding new strategies to stay on track.

Reflect on how you respond to unexpected changes. Are there ways to approach challenges with more openness and creativity? Embracing adaptability allows you to see obstacles as opportunities for growth rather than roadblocks.

Seeking Inspiration from Others

You're not alone in your struggles, and finding inspiration in the stories of others can remind you of what's possible. Whether it's reading about someone who overcame similar challenges, listening to motivational speakers, or connecting with a supportive community, these stories can fuel your determination and provide valuable insights.

Reflect on the people or stories that inspire you. Are there role models, mentors, or peers whose experiences resonate with your own?

Surrounding yourself with sources of encouragement can help you stay motivated.

Practicing Gratitude

Gratitude is a powerful antidote to negativity. Even in the face of challenges, taking time to acknowledge what's going well in your life can shift your perspective and boost your mood. Gratitude helps you focus on abundance rather than scarcity, reminding you of the progress you've made and the resources you have.

Reflect on three things you're grateful for today. How does focusing on these positives change the way you view your current challenges? Gratitude doesn't erase difficulties, but it helps you approach them from a place of strength and optimism.

Celebrating Small Wins

When progress feels slow, celebrating small victories can provide the encouragement you need to keep going. Each milestone, no matter how minor, represents a step in the right direction. Whether it's sticking to your budget for a month, making an extra loan payment, or saving a few extra dollars, these wins deserve recognition.

Reflect on your recent achievements. Are there moments of progress you've overlooked or taken for granted? Celebrating these wins reminds you that every effort counts and that you're moving forward, even if it doesn't always feel like it.

Leaning on Your Support System

During tough times, don't hesitate to lean on your support system. Whether it's family, friends, or a mentor, having someone to talk to can provide comfort, perspective, and practical advice. Sharing your struggles with trusted individuals reminds you that you're not alone and that help is available.

Reflect on the people in your life who support and encourage you. Are there opportunities to strengthen these connections or seek their guidance? Reaching out can make all the difference when challenges feel overwhelming.

Practicing Self-Compassion

It's easy to be hard on yourself when things don't go as planned, but self-compassion is essential for staying motivated. Acknowledge your efforts and recognize that setbacks are a natural part of any journey. Treat yourself with the same kindness and understanding you would offer a friend facing similar challenges.

Reflect on how you speak to yourself during difficult times. Are there ways to be more patient and forgiving with yourself? Practicing self-compassion helps you maintain a positive mindset and avoid unnecessary stress.

Staying Focused on the Bigger Picture

When challenges arise, it's important to zoom out and focus on the bigger picture. A single setback doesn't define your entire journey, and temporary difficulties don't erase the progress you've made. By keeping your long-term goals in mind, you can maintain perspective and avoid getting discouraged by short-term setbacks.

Reflect on the larger purpose behind your efforts. How does this challenge fit into the overall context of your journey? Staying focused on the big picture helps you navigate difficulties with resilience and determination.

Building Momentum Through Action

Sometimes, the best way to overcome a challenge is simply to take action. Even small steps, like revising your budget, reaching out for advice, or setting a new goal, can create momentum and help you regain a sense of control. Action transforms feelings of helplessness into empowerment, reminding you of your ability to influence outcomes.

Reflect on one action you can take today to move forward. How might this small step help you regain confidence and motivation? Each action builds momentum, bringing you closer to your goals.

Reflecting on Your Journey

Challenges are an inevitable part of growth, but they also provide opportunities to learn, adapt, and become stronger. Reflecting on your journey as a whole can help you appreciate how far you've come and remind you of your resilience. Each obstacle you overcome adds to your story of success, proving that you have what it takes to keep pushing forward.

Reflect on the challenges you've faced in the past and how you've grown as a result. What strengths have you developed, and how can you apply them to your current situation? You've already shown incredible determination, and you're capable of continuing to rise above any obstacle.

You're stronger than any challenge that comes your way, and your determination will carry you through even the toughest times. Keep going—you're building a future that's worth every effort, and every step forward brings you closer to achieving your dreams. You've got this!

Chapter 14

The Bigger Picture of Financial Empowerment

Changing the Narrative for Black Women

The narrative surrounding Black women and wealth has often been one of struggle, resilience, and overcoming systemic barriers. While those qualities speak to immense strength and determination, they don't define the full picture. Black women are powerful agents of change, capable of rewriting the story to one of abundance, financial security, and generational wealth. Saving and wealth-building aren't just acts of personal empowerment—they're tools for dismantling outdated narratives, reclaiming agency, and redefining what's possible for yourself and your community.

Breaking Free from Limiting Beliefs

For many Black women, societal and cultural narratives have perpetuated limiting beliefs about money and success. These beliefs, often rooted in historical injustices and systemic inequities, can create barriers to dreaming bigger and pursuing financial goals with confidence. However, these narratives don't have to dictate your future. You have the power to challenge and rewrite them, starting with how you view yourself and your potential.

Reflect on the messages about money and success you've internalized over the years. Were there moments when you doubted your ability to achieve financial security or wealth? Recognizing these patterns is the first step toward breaking free from them. Your worth and capability extend far beyond any limiting belief.

Redefining Wealth for Yourself

Wealth isn't just about material possessions or large bank accounts—it's about freedom, security, and the ability to create opportunities for yourself and others. For Black women, redefining wealth means shifting the focus from survival to thriving. It's about building a financial foundation that allows you to live fully, pursue your dreams, and leave a legacy for future generations.

Reflect on what wealth means to you. Is it the ability to travel, start a business, or provide for your family without worry? Defining wealth on your own terms helps you set goals that align with your values and aspirations.

Saving as an Act of Empowerment

Saving money isn't just a practical step—it's a radical act of empowerment. It's a way of saying, "I deserve security, freedom, and choices." For Black women, who have often been excluded from wealth-building opportunities, saving is a tool for reclaiming agency and asserting control over your financial future.

Reflect on how saving has changed your perspective. Has it given you a sense of control, pride, or confidence? Recognizing the power of saving reinforces its importance in your journey toward financial empowerment.

Building Wealth Against the Odds

The systemic barriers that have historically limited access to wealth for Black women are real, but so is your ability to overcome them. By embracing tools like education, investing, entrepreneurship, and community support, you're carving out pathways to success that weren't always available.

Reflect on the challenges you've faced in your financial journey. How have you navigated those obstacles, and what have you learned from them? Each step forward is a testament to your strength and determination.

Inspiring Future Generations

When Black women build wealth, the impact extends far beyond the individual. It creates a ripple effect, inspiring future generations to dream bigger and pursue financial goals with confidence. By saving and investing, you're not just creating opportunities for yourself—you're paving the way for others to follow.

Reflect on the legacy you want to leave for your family or community. How can your journey inspire others to believe in their own potential? Sharing your story is a powerful way to amplify your impact and uplift those around you.

Challenging Systemic Barriers Through Wealth

Wealth-building is more than a personal journey—it's a way to challenge systemic inequities and push for broader change. When Black women achieve financial success, they gain the resources and influence needed to advocate for policies that promote equity, create opportunities, and dismantle barriers.

Reflect on how your financial empowerment aligns with your values and desire for change. Are there ways to use your resources to support causes or initiatives that matter to you? Building wealth isn't just about individual gain—it's about collective progress.

Celebrating the New Narrative

The narrative surrounding Black women and wealth is evolving. Today, Black women are leading businesses, investing in communities, and achieving milestones that were once considered out of reach. By prioritizing saving and wealth-building, you're contributing to this new story—one of possibility, resilience, and success.

Reflect on how your journey fits into this broader narrative. How does your progress redefine what's possible for yourself and others? Celebrating your achievements is a reminder of how far you've come and the impact you're making.

Reflecting on Your Role in the Narrative

You are part of a larger movement of Black women reshaping the story of financial empowerment. Your efforts to save, invest, and build wealth contribute to a legacy of strength and resilience that transcends generations. Reflect on the pride and purpose that come with being a changemaker in your own life and beyond.

Inspiring Others to Save

Your financial journey is more than a personal endeavor—it has the power to influence and uplift those around you. When you share your experiences, challenges, and triumphs, you become a source of encouragement and inspiration for your community. Saving is not just about achieving personal goals; it's about creating a ripple effect that helps others recognize their potential and take steps toward their own financial empowerment.

The Power of Leading by Example

One of the most effective ways to inspire others is to lead by example. When people see your commitment to saving and witness the results of your efforts, it challenges them to reimagine what's possible for themselves. Sharing your journey authentically—your successes, setbacks, and lessons learned—makes the idea of saving relatable and achievable.

Reflect on how your actions have influenced those around you. Have friends, family, or coworkers commented on your financial discipline or asked for advice? These moments highlight the power of your example and the impact you're already making.

Sharing Your Story Authentically

Every financial journey is unique, and your story carries value simply because it's yours. Whether you've overcome debt, built an emergency fund, or achieved a major savings goal, your experience can serve as a roadmap for others. Sharing your story authentically—without embellishment or judgment—creates a connection that resonates deeply.

Reflect on the milestones and challenges that have shaped your journey. What insights have you gained that could benefit others? Your honesty and vulnerability can make your story more impactful, inspiring others to take the first step toward their goals.

Encouraging Conversations About Money

For many, talking about money feels uncomfortable or taboo. By initiating conversations about saving and financial empowerment, you help break down these barriers and create a space for open dialogue. Sharing tips, discussing strategies, or simply expressing your enthusiasm for saving can spark interest and motivate others to explore their own financial habits.

Reflect on how you approach money conversations. Are there ways to make them more inclusive or engaging? Your willingness to talk about saving can normalize the topic and encourage others to join the conversation.

Providing Practical Tips and Tools

While sharing your journey is inspiring, offering practical advice can make it actionable. Whether it's a budgeting method that worked for you, an app you've found helpful, or a specific savings strategy, these tools provide a starting point for those who may not know where to begin.

Reflect on the resources and techniques that have been most effective for you. How can you share them in a way that feels accessible and encouraging? Equipping others with tools and knowledge empowers them to take control of their finances.

Celebrating the Wins of Others

Inspiring others isn't just about your own journey—it's also about celebrating the progress and achievements of those around you. Acknowledging and supporting their efforts reinforces positive habits and builds a sense of community. Whether it's a friend saving for a vacation or a coworker paying off debt, your encouragement can make a lasting impact.

Reflect on the ways you uplift others in their financial journeys. Are there opportunities to celebrate their wins more openly or consistently? Celebrating together strengthens the bond between your journey and theirs.

Building a Community of Support

Saving is easier when you have a support system. By fostering a community where people can share their goals, challenges, and successes, you create an environment of accountability and encouragement. This could be a small group of friends, a social media platform, or a larger community initiative.

Reflect on the support systems in your life. Could you create or contribute to a community focused on financial empowerment? Building these connections amplifies the impact of your journey and inspires collective progress.

Overcoming Resistance and Skepticism

Not everyone will be immediately receptive to conversations about saving. Some may feel it's impossible given their current circumstances, while others may be skeptical about the benefits. Addressing these concerns with empathy and understanding can help shift their perspective.

Reflect on the resistance you've encountered in your own journey. How can you use those experiences to relate to others and offer encouragement? Recognizing and validating their feelings creates a foundation for meaningful dialogue.

Inspiring Across Generations

Your influence isn't limited to your peers—it extends to future generations as well. By modeling healthy financial habits and sharing your knowledge, you set a powerful example for younger family members or community members. Teaching children and teens the value of saving instills habits that can shape their financial futures.

Reflect on the younger people in your life. Are there ways to involve them in your saving journey or teach them about money management? Your guidance can leave a lasting impact on their relationship with finances.

Amplifying Your Impact Through Advocacy

Sharing your journey can go beyond personal interactions. Advocacy—whether through writing, public speaking, or social media—amplifies your message and reaches a broader audience. By sharing your story publicly, you inspire people you may never meet and contribute to a larger movement of financial empowerment.

Reflect on platforms or opportunities where you could share your experiences more widely. Are there blogs, community events, or organizations that align with your mission? Expanding your reach increases the impact of your journey.

Reflecting on the Ripple Effect

Every time you inspire someone to save, you create a ripple effect that extends far beyond that individual. As they achieve their goals and share their journey, they inspire others in turn, creating a cycle of empowerment and progress.

Reflect on the potential ripple effects of your journey. How many lives could you touch simply by sharing your experiences and encouragement? Recognizing this impact reinforces the importance of your efforts.

Celebrating the Power of Collective Progress

Your journey is part of a larger movement toward financial empowerment within your community. By inspiring others to save, you contribute to a collective effort that strengthens families, neighborhoods, and generations to come. Together, these individual stories create a new narrative—one of possibility, resilience, and success.

Reflect on how your journey fits into this collective progress. How does inspiring others align with your own goals and values? Celebrating this shared momentum reminds you that your impact is far-reaching and significant.

Your Legacy of Financial Strength

Legacy is more than what you leave behind; it's the impact you create during your lifetime that resonates for generations. Through intentional saving and wealth-building, you have the power to leave a mark that extends far beyond material possessions. Your financial journey is not just about achieving personal milestones; it's about crafting a story of resilience, empowerment, and opportunity for those who come after you. Building a legacy of financial strength means creating a foundation that inspires, uplifts, and supports others while ensuring your values live on.

Understanding the Concept of Financial Legacy

A financial legacy is the culmination of your efforts to manage, grow, and pass on wealth in a way that reflects your values and priorities. It's about using your resources to shape the future for your family, community, or causes you care about. Your legacy doesn't have to involve massive wealth—it's about the intentional choices you make to create opportunities and security for others.

Reflect on what financial legacy means to you. Is it about ensuring your children have access to education, supporting your community, or contributing to a cause close to your heart? Defining your legacy helps you align your actions with your vision for the future.

Building a Legacy Through Intentional Saving

Saving is the cornerstone of financial strength, and it plays a vital role in building your legacy. By consistently setting aside resources, you're creating a safety net that provides stability during uncertainties and opportunities for growth. Intentional saving isn't just about accumulating money—it's about laying the groundwork for long-term impact.

Reflect on how your saving habits have evolved over time. Are there areas where you could be more intentional about allocating resources toward your legacy goals? Small, consistent efforts can lead to significant results over time.

Generational Wealth and Its Impact

Generational wealth is one of the most tangible ways to leave a lasting impact. It's about passing down assets—such as property, investments, or businesses—that provide financial stability and opportunities for your family. But it's also about sharing the knowledge and values that empower future generations to sustain and grow that wealth.

Reflect on the legacy you've inherited, if any, and how it has shaped your financial journey. Are there lessons or resources you wish had been passed down to you? These reflections can guide your approach to building and preserving generational wealth.

Educating and Empowering the Next Generation

A critical part of leaving a legacy is equipping the next generation with the tools and knowledge they need to succeed. Teaching your children or younger family members about money management, saving, and investing ensures they can make informed decisions and continue building on the foundation you've created.

Reflect on how you can incorporate financial education into your legacy. Are there ways to make these lessons engaging and relatable for younger family members? Empowering the next generation with knowledge is one of the most meaningful gifts you can give.

Investing in Your Community

Your financial legacy doesn't have to be limited to your family—it can also extend to your community. By supporting local initiatives, funding scholarships, or contributing to community projects, you're investing in the collective progress of those around you. These actions create a ripple effect, spreading the benefits of your efforts far and wide.

Reflect on the causes or organizations that align with your values. How can your resources be used to make a meaningful impact? Investing in your community ensures your legacy is both personal and far-reaching.

Aligning Your Legacy With Your Values

Your legacy is a reflection of who you are and what you stand for. By aligning your financial decisions with your values, you ensure that your wealth serves a purpose beyond material gain. Whether it's supporting social justice, promoting education, or protecting the environment, intentional wealth-building allows you to contribute to the causes that matter most to you.

Reflect on the values that guide your financial decisions. Are there ways to incorporate these values more explicitly into your saving and wealth-building strategies? A value-driven legacy resonates more deeply and leaves a lasting impression.

Planning for the Future

Creating a financial legacy requires careful planning. This includes setting clear goals, creating an estate plan, and ensuring that your wishes are documented and legally protected. Working with financial advisors, estate planners, or attorneys can help you navigate the complexities of passing on wealth and ensuring it's used in the way you intend.

Reflect on your current plans for the future. Have you taken steps to formalize your legacy through wills, trusts, or other tools? Planning ahead provides peace of mind and ensures your legacy is secure.

Overcoming Challenges and Barriers

Building a financial legacy isn't without its challenges. Systemic barriers, unexpected life events, and personal setbacks can all impact your ability to save and build wealth. But resilience, adaptability, and a clear sense of purpose can help you navigate these obstacles and stay focused on your goals.

Reflect on the challenges you've faced in your financial journey. How have they shaped your perspective and approach? Overcoming these challenges adds depth and meaning to your legacy.

Celebrating Progress and Honoring Your Journey

As you work toward creating a legacy of financial strength, take time to celebrate your progress and honor the journey you've undertaken. Every milestone, no matter how small, represents a step closer to achieving your vision. Acknowledging your efforts reinforces the importance of your mission and keeps you motivated to continue.

Reflect on the achievements that have brought you closer to your legacy goals. How can you honor these moments in a way that inspires you and those around you? Celebrating your progress is a reminder of the impact you're creating.

Reflecting on the Bigger Picture

Your financial legacy is part of a larger story—one of resilience, empowerment, and progress. By saving intentionally and building wealth with purpose, you're not just securing your own future; you're contributing to a broader movement of empowerment and opportunity. Your efforts today will resonate for years to come, shaping the lives of those who follow in your footsteps.

Reflect on the story you want your legacy to tell. How does your journey contribute to the greater narrative of progress and possibility? Your legacy is a testament to your strength, vision, and commitment to creating a better future.

Conclusion

Your Journey to Financial Freedom

As you reach the end of this book, take a moment to reflect on how far you've come. This isn't just about the financial milestones you've achieved or the knowledge you've gained—it's about the mindset you've cultivated and the confidence you've built along the way. Your journey to financial freedom is a testament to your strength, determination, and commitment to creating a brighter future.

Reflecting on Your Growth

Think back to where you started. Maybe saving felt overwhelming, or the idea of building wealth seemed out of reach. Now, you've taken steps to understand your financial situation, set goals, and make intentional choices that align with your values. Those choices, no matter how small, have laid the foundation for a lifetime of empowerment and opportunity.

Reflect on your proudest moments throughout this journey. Was it the first time you hit a savings milestone? Or perhaps the realization that you could overcome a financial challenge that once felt insurmountable? Celebrating these moments isn't just about looking back—it's about honoring the progress that will fuel your path forward.

A Bright Future Awaits

Your financial journey is far from over, but the progress you've made sets the stage for what's to come. With each step, you've built habits and knowledge that will serve you for years to come. More than that, you've proven to yourself that you have what it takes to achieve your goals, no matter how ambitious they may be.

Imagine the future you're creating. Picture the security of an emergency fund, the freedom to pursue passions without financial fear, and the joy of watching your wealth grow over time. Reflect on how this vision aligns with your deepest values and aspirations. This isn't just a dream—it's a future you're actively shaping with every choice you make.

Encouragement to Keep Going

There will be times when the path feels difficult. Setbacks might arise, and progress might seem slow. In those moments, remember that every small step counts. Each dollar saved, each goal achieved, and each habit strengthened brings you closer to the life you envision.

Remind yourself why you started. Was it to create stability for your family? To free yourself from financial stress? To leave a legacy for future generations? Whatever your "why" may be, hold onto it as a source of motivation and inspiration. You're not just working toward financial freedom—you're proving to yourself that you're capable of achieving anything you set your mind to.

Practical Next Steps

As you move forward, consider how you'll maintain the momentum you've built. Financial freedom is a journey, not a destination, and staying focused on your goals requires intention and planning. Here are some practical steps to keep your progress on track:

Regularly Review Your Goals: Life changes, and so do your priorities. Make it a habit to review your financial goals periodically, adjusting them as needed to ensure they align with your evolving needs and dreams.

Celebrate Milestones: Acknowledge the progress you make along the way, whether it's paying off a debt, reaching a savings target, or achieving a personal financial victory. Celebrating keeps you motivated and reminds you of the bigger picture.

Continue Learning: The more you learn about money management, investing, and wealth-building, the more empowered you'll feel. Seek out resources, attend workshops, or connect with mentors who can help you expand your knowledge.

Plan for the Long Term: Think beyond the immediate future and consider how your choices today will shape the years ahead. Whether it's contributing to retirement accounts, exploring investment opportunities, or building generational wealth, long-term planning ensures your efforts have lasting impact.

Reflect on which of these steps resonate most with you. How can you incorporate them into your routine to keep building on the foundation you've created? Taking action ensures that your journey doesn't end here—it continues to grow and evolve.

Your Journey Is Unique

No two financial journeys look the same, and that's what makes yours so powerful. Your story is shaped by your experiences, goals, and values, and it carries the potential to inspire others. By embracing your uniqueness and staying true to your purpose, you're not only achieving financial freedom for yourself—you're redefining what's possible for those who look up to you.

Reflect on how your journey has influenced those around you. Have friends, family, or coworkers been inspired by your progress? Sharing your story can create a ripple effect of empowerment, spreading the message that financial freedom is attainable for everyone.

The Power of Persistence

As you continue your journey, remember that persistence is key. Financial freedom isn't about perfection—it's about progress. There will be days when sticking to your plan feels challenging, but those are the moments when your commitment matters most. By staying focused on your goals and remaining flexible in your approach, you'll overcome obstacles and keep moving forward.

Reflect on the challenges you've faced and the resilience you've shown. How can you draw on those experiences to navigate future difficulties? Each challenge is an opportunity to grow stronger and more confident in your abilities.

A Legacy of Empowerment

Your financial journey isn't just about you—it's about the legacy you're creating for others. Whether it's teaching your children about money, supporting your community, or inspiring peers to take control of their finances, your efforts have a far-reaching impact. By prioritizing saving, building wealth, and sharing your knowledge, you're contributing to a movement of empowerment and progress.

Reflect on the legacy you want to leave behind. What values do you hope to pass on, and how can you use your journey to inspire others? Your story has the power to shape lives and create lasting change.

Looking Ahead

The end of this book marks the beginning of a new chapter in your financial journey. You've gained tools, insights, and strategies to take control of your finances, but the true power lies in your ability to take action. Every step you take, no matter how small, brings you closer to the life you envision.

Reflect on the next steps you'll take to continue your journey. Are there goals you're ready to tackle, habits you want to strengthen, or challenges you're prepared to face? The future is yours to create, and your efforts today are shaping the possibilities of tomorrow.

You've Got This

You've shown that you have the determination, resilience, and vision to achieve financial freedom. The journey isn't always easy, but it's worth every effort. Trust in your ability to make intentional choices, embrace opportunities, and overcome challenges. You have everything you need to succeed—and more.

As you move forward, carry this message with you: You are capable, deserving, and unstoppable. Financial freedom is within your reach, and your journey is a testament to the strength and potential you hold. Keep going—you've got this!

Made in the USA
Monee, IL
04 November 2026

67381360R10105